In honor of my son Ashwin, The Pursuit
is dedicated to him realizing his American
and personal dreams and living life to the fullest.

In honor of my dad, Ganesan,
and mother, Dhavanmani Devi,
for taking the risk with their life savings.
They sent me to America to pursue the
American dream and the dream of my life.

"I hope this manifesto will restore the pen to its former glory, so I wrote it. I cannot think of a better reason than to use the pen to help reunite our nation. Along with promoting the American Dream, keeping Americans united, and encouraging them to pursue their happiness, I want to usher in a new generation of entrepreneurs, dreamers, and social entrepreneurs.

-Tel Ganesan
Serial Entrepreneur and Global Humanitarian

The Pursuit

A Manifesto by Tel Ganesan

Published by Kyyba Media
ISBN: 9781087924199
Copyright 2022 by Tel Ganesan
www.theamericandreamguru.com

CONTENTS

PREFACE

I against my brother.
I and my brother against my cousin.
I, my brother, and my cousin against the world.
-Old Bedouin Proverb

Throughout most of recorded history, humans have lived in tribes. This allowed them to share resources, support each other, and work together to ensure their survival. As a result, humans have been able to form communities with shared values. Develop traditions, and ways of life that have passed down through generations.

This is like a quilt, with each strand representing an individual in the tribe and the general pattern formed through their combined effort. Each person adds to the culture and to society. They weave individual contributions into a larger pattern that is greater than the sum of its parts. This collective effort contributes to the vibrancy of the tribe. The individual threads of each person create a beautiful design.

Tribes

Tribes have built and maintained culture and society through this concept of collective effort. This idea of contributing to the collective creates a sense of belonging and purpose, which helps to build a strong sense of community.

It has always been this way for tribes to provide comfort, pride, and a means of defending their groups from their rivals. Thus, they place such a strong emphasis on tribal loyalty and unity. In times of strife and danger, it was important that tribes had a unified front in order to defend themselves from outside forces.

This was especially true in days before modern weapons and technology, when physical strength and loyalty were the only thing a tribe had to rely on for protection.

In order to ensure their protection and maintain their group identity, tribes developed complex social structures and cultural practices. Because of generations of passing down these practices, we still practice them today.

According to science, we can store memories in our genes for up to fourteen generations. As a result, it ingrained tribalism in our DNA.

In a chaotic world, tribes gave people a name and social significance. It made the environment much less confusing and dangerous. Regardless of one's background, everyone needs a tribe, a group formed to fight for power and territory, to demonize the enemy, to plan rallies and raise flags.

Since human nature has not changed, modern groups are like ancient tribes. In fact, these groups are direct descendants of primitive humans. The technological and social advances of modern society haven't changed our instinctual need to connect with others. Human beings have always needed connection and to feel like we belong. It is a testament to the basic need for companionship. Humans still want to form meaningful relationships, even in a digital world.

People can now connect in ways that were not possible before social media. Social media has provided an outlet for people to express themselves and their ideas, as well as to form meaningful relationships with others. Social media has become a powerful tool to build communities of people from all walks of life connecting them and allowing them to share experiences and grow together. For example, online support groups allow people to discuss personal and social issues in a safe and supportive environment, creating a sense of belonging and reducing feelings of isolation.

The Paradox

It is ironic that the things that bring us together are also the things that separate us. This paradox of togetherness and separateness is a source of great tension and mistrust between different groups. We often see this manifested in our culture as people who share a common culture, language, and differences in lifestyle, beliefs, and opinions can still divide values. This creates a divide that can be difficult to bridge and can lead to feelings of mistrust and animosity.

In order to have a successful society within a tribal setting, there must be a certain level of trust between the members. We must earn this trust and can achieve it by practicing cooperation and understanding the dynamics of the group. Teachers must teach children the rules of survival in order to thrive in a tribal setting, such as forming alliances, understanding the nuances of inter-group relations, and being able to read social cues. Without these skills, it is difficult to survive in a tribal setting. In a tribe, you will grow up surrounded by enemies.

Tribes To Authoritarianism

Fast forward to now. Authoritarianism is spreading like a virus. Because of social media platforms, distrust and disgust are being generated. Distrust at much deeper levels than ever possible in human history. Each of the two political parties believes itself to be so pure. In their opinion, there are only two viable tribes: liberals or conservatives.

This tribalism has resulted in a polarized and hostile environment, where it is difficult to find common ground to build trust between the two sides. This has the potential to lead to further conflict, as neither side will compromise, with each side intent on protecting their own interests. The pandemic has forced both sides to retreat into their corners of fear. It is clear from both, that they feel an enemy is trying to take what is rightfully theirs.

This fear leads to a breakdown in communication and a lack of trust in each other, which can further escalate into an already tense situation. It can also lead to a lack of cooperation, which can prevent progress from being made in resolving the conflict. This fear can contribute to an increase in militarization and an increase in violence, which can further destabilize the region. To gain political power, two entrenched tribes can spread division and hatred among the American people. Their aim is to force us to choose either Red or Blue, with hatred accompanying this choice towards the opposing tribe. Hatred comes at the expense of the greater good of our nation. Hatred becomes an existential threat to our nation. Extremism is rampant and only gets more extreme. People are moving further toward either end of the spectrum instead of leaders speaking out. As a result, they pose a threat to the American way of life and to democracy.

The Dream

My success living in the American Dream is the reason for writing this manifesto. As a student, I came to America. I've been fortunate to enjoy many successes. A career as an engineer, as an entrepreneur, and am now as a serial entrepreneur. The pursuit of happiness in the land of freedom has changed my life and that of my children. I've experienced a noble life, one of diversity, creativity, innovation and disruption. Because of my financial wealth, I am sought after by both political tribes. In America, the unifying color is green, so if we own money, either blue or red want us.

My financial success has given me the opportunity and resources to explore a variety of interests. As an engineer and an entrepreneur, I have been able to create and grow successful businesses. I have also been able to use my financial wealth to bridge the political divide in the United States. We see money as a unifying factor despite partisan differences.

For example, I have been able to donate to both Republican and Democratic candidates in order to encourage dialogue and understanding between the two parties. This has enabled me to use my resources to make a positive impact on the political landscape by supporting candidates and initiatives that promote cooperation across the aisle. In addition, I have provided financial help to causes and organizations bridging the political divide.

The Challenge Ahead

The challenge facing our nation is saving American democracy and our way of life. I believe saving democracy is possible.

It's my hope for America that we will move into the future as one, despite our cultural differences. We can help raise each other's awareness. Democracy brings us a promise. Let's move forward together on that promise. We can bridge the gap between our differences by engaging in open dialogue and by understanding each other's perspectives.

We need to work together to create a fairer society and ensure that everyone has a voice. By recognizing the value of diversity and its power to enrich our nation, we can ensure that American democracy remains strong and vibrant for future générations.

By developing a shared understanding of our core values, we can together create a better future for all. We can achieve this through open dialogue and understanding of other perspectives, as well as advocating for policies that promote equity and inclusion. By understanding our shared values and working together, we can create a more unified society, which will lead to greater progress and prosperity. For example, advocating for policies that promote access to education for all, regardless of financial background, is an important step towards a more fair and just society.

Different cultures and viewpoints can work in harmony based on our larger shared national identity for the greater good. Manifestos like this one can aid in the fight. As Henry Kimsey-House, Co-Active Leadership: Five Ways to Lead, wrote: "Our differences need not divide us because even as we are unique and individual, we are also all one."

It is the people of the United States of America of which I am proud to be a citizen. This journey has brought me everything I ever dreamed of.

We come into life with nothing, and we leave with nothing. With my financial dreams having come true, now I turn my attention to helping others pursue happiness.

I urge you to fight a worthy fight of understanding universal consciousness and establishing connections. If our minds are open to possibilities, we can build a magnificent future. The American Dream unites us, and all things are possible if our hearts and minds decide to make it happen. Together, we can tap into this potential and make our collective dreams come true.

Massive social impact will transform the country and solve societal problems. With the power of collective consciousness and a unified sense of purpose, we work together to create real, lasting change. We can tackle systemic issues, bridge divides, and create a society that works for everyone. We must keep our eyes on our shared vision of a brighter future and take steps towards making it a reality.

Tel Ganesan
Serial Entrepreneur and
Global Humanitarian

INTRODUCTION

"The best argument against democracy is a
five-minute conversation with the average voter."
- Winston Churchill

In a democracy, people choose their rulers, which makes it the best form of government. It ensures that power lies in the hands of the people, allowing them to be in full control of their lives. In a democracy, people may vote, which gives them a say in who their leaders are and what policies they implement. This means that people can choose their own destiny, as opposed to having it dictated to them by a ruler or a governing body. It allows people to have a say in the laws and regulations that affect their lives, thus protecting their rights and freedoms. For instance, if the majority of the population votes in favor of a law that gives them greater freedom of speech, thus protecting their rights.

Our democracy depends on every one of us. Together, we can protect it. By joining, not just in solidarity, but in action, we can ensure that our democracy remains strong and intact. When we unite, our collective voice can push for meaningful policy changes and to hold our elected officials accountable. We can cause an impact and to guarantee that we protect our democracy.

Voters will not re-elect leaders who do not perform well. There is more freedom of speech in democracy than in any other form of government.

This ensures that we hear the voices of the people, enabling them to hold their leaders accountable for their decisions and actions. The people can vote out leaders who cannot perform to their expectations in a democratic system. This allows the people to have a say toward their government and ensures that they hold the leader to the highest standard. All of us must work together to defeat authoritarianism. To achieve this, we must collaborate and harness the power of our collective voices. Let's work together to reverse the tide of authoritarianism in America.

Democracies, monarchies, oligarchies, authoritarian regimes, and totalitarian regimes are other political systems. Such systems are based on varying levels of control, with democracy providing the most freedom and totalitarianism providing the least. Democracies provide the most freedom because they are based on the principle of majority rule, and they shared the power between the governing body and the   people.

In a monarchy, the concentrated power is in the hands of the monarch and their authority is absolute. Oligarchies are similar, but the power is held by a small group of people, rather than one individual. Authoritarian regimes have a centralized power structure, where the government controls all aspects of life. Totalitarian regimes are the most oppressive and the most extreme form of authoritarianism, where the government has complete control over the people.

Since authoritarian regimes lack legitimate authority, their leaders are more prone to political instability. As a result, totalitarians often resort to fear-mongering tactics to maintain their power and control. Such regimes lack any popular support or legitimacy from the people, so they must rely on coercive tactics to maintain their power. This can often lead to increased repression, censorship, and the use of propaganda to control public opinion.

Why is democracy declining around the world? This alarming trend of democratic decline is leading to an unsettling rise in authoritarianism and intolerant regimes around the globe.

Combining factors, such as populism, weakening of civil society and political institutions, erosion of public trust in government, and the decline of the rule of law, is causing this decline. These factors contribute to the decline of democracy in many countries.

There is a threat to the freedom of the world, not just from the rise of autocracies, but also from the faltering of major democracies. Autocratic governments are using their power to stifle the voices of their own citizens, as well as those of their neighbors. Major democracies are struggling to maintain their economies.

This is leading to a rise in populism and weakening commitments to the rule of law and civil liberties. This is creating a dangerous global environment, as the ideals of democracy, freedom, and justice are under threat.

My mission is one of collective empowerment and understanding. One grounded in the powerful sentiment that, if when we unite our energy and intentions, we can create a world where anything is possible. We can also draw on the strength of the American Dream to motivate us, as well as the understanding that by coming together, we can create a brighter future for all.

THE MISSION

"The seed to the solution is always in the problem
if we look deep within."
-Tel Ganesan
Serial Entrepreneur and Global Humanitarian

The Mission of The American Dream Guru

My primary aim is to reunite our nation. To achieve this goal, we must put aside our differences and come together as one.
A famous saying by Aesop: "United we stand, divided we fall." This manifesto aims to remind us of the core values that unite us as Americans, regardless of our political affiliations. We must not forget that, for our   nation, we are all in this together.

This manifesto should also help to heal the divide in the United States of America.

By uniting citizens through shared values of acceptance and understanding, we can bridge this gap and create a nation that is stronger than ever.

America is the land of opportunity. The founders of America had the foresight to give us these three tenants: "Life, Liberty and the Pursuit of Happiness." One can have all the material things in the world, but if you are not happy, it means nothing.

The founders of America recognized these three tenants were essential for a person to pursue their dreams and reach their full potential. It is these three that allow people to have the freedom to pursue a life of their choosing. This allows them satisfaction with where they are in life. It's a continuous journey. In my mind happiness is the mother of all goals. The pursuit of happiness gives us the chance to live a fulfilling life. We should pursue the pursuit!

We are all equal in this pursuit because of the constitution. That's the American dream. By having the freedom to pursue their goals, individuals have the chance to work hard and develop their skills in order to achieve success.

This is important for both individuals and society, as it can help to foster economic growth and create a more fair and prosperous society. We are all equal in this pursuit because of the constitution.

Truth Matters

We live in a world where disinformation is spreading. Disinformation spreads more easily than facts because of biases in our information ecosystem. Citizens cannot trust each other or our political leaders in a democracy without shared facts. Our political two-party system has divided us for decades for a myriad of reasons. By spreading false information, bad-faith actors threaten to turn too many of us apathetic, or even hostile, towards democratic institutions. Together, we can create a healthier political discourse based on shared facts, honest disagreement, and honest differences of opinion.

We can protect the Declaration of Independence, ensuring that our right to life, liberty, and pursuit of happiness remains, and that we can fight against the divisions that threaten to tear apart our democracy and undermine our two-party system.

This manifesto bridges the divide between us. We must come together to ensure that we hear all voices. To do this, we must listen to and understand each other, despite our differences. As Martin Luther King Jr. once said: "In the end, we will remember not the words of our enemies, but the silence of our friends."

Whether we are Democrats or Republicans, we need to identify first as Americans. This can help us come together as a nation enabling us to move forward and achieve progress for all. Political parties may have different philosophies, but we are all citizens of the same nation.

We need to come together and put aside our differences in order to build a better country for ourselves and our children...

I want this manifesto to help heal the divide that exists in the United States of America. Reunification of our nation is our primary goal. This book seeks to remind   us of the core values that unite us as Americans, regardless of our political affiliations. By understanding and embracing our shared identity, we can bridge the gap that our political differences have created and strive for a more unified nation.

One thing you must do is not surround yourself with negative people because, for some, their pursuit of the American dream is on the inside. You must remain flexible so you can adapt and keep making changes so you can pursue. We all fight the same demons.

You must raise your awareness level. Whatever you do, you must do it with intention and do it with passion. To generate original ideas and thoughts, everyone strives to maintain a positive mental attitude. Leads to actions, and actions lead to success. Happiness is the key to success. We should pursue the pursuit!

In moving America forward together, democracy brings us from different cultures and viewpoints to a place where we can come together for a worthy cause. It is based on our shared national identity. Through democracy, we can find common ground and recognize that, although we have different ideas, we share the same core values and beliefs. This allows us to compromise and come up with solutions that benefit all Americans. Plato, the ancient Greek philosopher, once wrote: "Democracy... is a charming form of government, full of variety and disorder; and dispensing a sort of equality to equals and un-equals alike."

It is only through hope and possibility that democracy can flourish. Creating an atmosphere of hope and possibility is essential to ensure the success of democracy and counter oppression authoritarianism presents. The most important tools we have are our optimism, willingness to trust and collaborate, openness to possibility, and strength in diversity. Democracy is, at its core, nothing less and nothing more than the conviction that, together, we can build a better world than any of us could design on our own.

Free and Fair Elections

As Americans, we exercise our political power most significantly through voting. We safeguard our voting rights and conduct our elections in a transparent and impartial manner to protect the integrity of our democracy. For example, the voting process should be secure and accessible, with measures in place to ensure that all votes are counted.

Elections should be free, fair, efficient, and secure for every eligible citizen. To ensure this, they must put safeguards in place to protect against voter fraud and ensure that we hear all voices. This includes measures such as implementing voter ID laws establishing secure election systems and providing access to polling locations for all eligible citizens. Such safeguards can help to ensure that only eligible citizens are voting, and that we counted their votes.

There are many challenges facing the American election system, including persistent barriers to voting for excluded communities and unprecedented threats to voting rights.

For instance, states have restricted registration and voting opportunities, passed voter ID laws, and implemented other barriers that impact people of color and other marginalized communities. In addition, gerrymandering has further limited the ability of the excluded to take part in the electoral process reducing their political power and representation.

We should strive for a strong and modern voting system that increases voter engagement and confidence. For instance, requiring all states to institute ranked-choice voting would enable voters to more accurately express their preferences and ensure that the winner of an election has the support of a majority of voters. This would also help to reduce the influence of money in politics, as candidates would no longer need to focus on appealing to the limited number of swing voters.

Responsible Representative Government

Democracies depend on governments that represent the interests of the people - those that will act on our behalf and hold them accountable when they do not. Therefore, it is so important for citizens to participate in their government; it is their voice that will ensure that their interests are being heard.

Democracies must have sound systems of checks and balances so that citizens can challenge the government when they feel their interests are not being represented. This helps to ensure that governments remain accountable to the people they serve.

Extreme polarization and institutional decline have caused government dysfunction and gridlock. As a result, it is important to ensure that government policies respond to citizens' needs and concerns.

For instance, the government has enacted laws that prioritize the interests of citizens in areas such as healthcare, education, and the environment. The first law in the Bill of Rights is the First Amendment, which protects citizens' rights to freedom of religion, speech, and the press, and the right to assemble and petition the government. By protecting citizens' rights, the government is ensuring that citizens have the power to make their voices heard and to hold their elected officials accountable. This helps to ensure that public policy responds to   citizens' needs and concerns and that the government can address the issues that matter most to citizens.

Governing in the interests of the American people requires powerful institutions and principled leadership. Therefore, it is essential that citizens empower themselves to ensure they hold their leaders to account. Citizens should vote and educate themselves about their leaders' decisions and policies. Citizens should have the tools and resources to make their voices heard and challenge the status quo if needed. This will ensure that American citizens have a say in who governs them and that we hold their leaders accountable for their decisions.

Diverse Public Square

Americans should have access to news and information they need to take part in civic life without fear of harassment or censorship, no matter where they live or who they are. They deserve to have their voices heard and to be informed about events that shape the world around them. This is especially true in a democracy, where citizens should be able to make informed decisions about who represents them and how their government is functioning.

Access to news and information allows citizens to hold leaders accountable and ensure that we heard their voices. For example, having access to accurate information about the current state of the economy can help citizens decide about whom to vote for in an election and how they should use their resources in the best way possible.

Our communities face new challenges and opportunities as the media landscape develops. To maximize our potential, we must adapt to these changes and use them to our advantage. We must make sure that we are staying up to date with the latest technology and trends, as well as utilizing the data that is available to us to inform our decisions and strategies. This will help us stay competitive and ensure that we are taking advantage of the opportunities that come with new media.

Providing trustworthy local news and investigative reporting, more fair newsrooms, press freedom, community engagement, and digital spaces that promote democracy are important. Emphasizing these efforts is essential to the health of a thriving democracy. Without these efforts, citizens cannot make informed decisions about the issues that affect their lives or hold their local, state, and national leaders accountable. Without a free press citizens cannot trust what information they receive, which can lead to a less informed electorate and a less healthy democracy.

With This Manifesto I Urge You, Adopt the Following Simple Propositions:

We should resolve our differences by debating and finding solutions.

We need to transcend tribalism and look for our commonalities. It's still our responsibility to fight for America and our democracy. Our ideals unite us, and we all recognize that we are Americans first!

We can be the agents of change, transforming our societies into more equal and just places. This is because, by joining forces and creating a collective effort, we can draw on a much wider range of experiences, skills, and resources to tackle the societal challenges we face. This shared pool of knowledge and resources allows us to make great strides in achieving meaningful and lasting change.

To safeguard democracy, every institution, and every one of us, must work together. Make use of your skills, strengths, profession, and community to do your part. By working together, we can strengthen our democracy and create lasting, meaningful change. We must work together to ensure that we protect our democracies' voices and make them heard. It is only through collective action that we can create a more just and fair society. If everyone does their part, then we can create a society that works for everyone.

Freedom is our ideal. Fight to save democracy by living in unity. #unitednotdivded #oneamerica #thepledge #supportveterans #freedomchallenge #fight-fordemocracy

Use the American Dream as a healing tool.
#americandreamlives

Use the Spirit of Entrepreneurship and the American Dream to help you pursue your happiness and heal the nation.
#beanentrepreneur #americandream

Understand that Pursuing Happiness leads to wellbe-ing, and wellbeing leads to   success. We relate well-ness to our pursuit of happiness
#thepursuitofhappiness #wellness

 Seek to create maximum social impact with kindness. We can change the land scape of our nation.
#createsocialimpact #americankindnes

DIVIDED NATION

e pluribus unum. "Out of many, One"
-National Motto

Divided Nation

Most Americans agree that democracy is in crisis and on the
verge of collapse. We must take decisive action now to prevent
the crisis from deepening. Many of the underlying issues that
have been festering for decades, such as systemic racism and
income inequality, have come to a head. These issues need to be
addressed in order to ensure the health and longevity of
democracy in the US.

Disclaimer: I am aware of the real, historical roots of our
differences. I will touch on the highlights but focus on the need
for Americans to develop a new and broader understanding of
democracy. As we seek to solve problems with others, we differ
from them and self-regulate. I aspire to a new brighter vision of
our possibilities, a country where we care for each other. To move
forward, we need to have a clear and open dialogue between
those with different views. We need to recognize that it is not just
about our differences, but about how we can learn from them,
come together and create solutions that benefit us all. A true
democracy is one that is based on mutual respect,
understanding, and cooperation. By acknowledging our
differences, we can create a brighter future together, one of
understanding, respect, and collaboration, that will lead to a
thriving democracy.

America faces a critical decision as the 2024 election approaches. The 2024 election guarantees a hyper-partisan war, with the American citizenry being bombarded with negative hate and fear-based advertising flooding the airwaves and social media platforms. This election could be a referendum on our country. It could determine whether the nation continues on its current path, or whether it shifts to a more progressive or conservative agenda. Including a defined problem with the probability of foreign actors paying to distribute propaganda with the intent to further divide. Who we listen to is our choice. Will we be patriots and recognize our call to action to protect our democracy?

The upcoming election will be a major determinant of the nation's future. It will be   an invaluable opportunity for citizens to decide how they want the government to address issues like foreign interference in elections. In addition, they can choose whether they want to choose a progressive or conservative direction. Citizens must decide how they will respond to this challenge and take action to protect our democratic institutions. Some say democracy is the worst form of government except for all the other forms that have been tried.

Will we be strong and move beyond political speech and cliquishness to reach out and connect with each other as Americans, without thought of political association? Important questions exist. Do we believe in the ideals set forth by the founders of this nation, such as democracy, civility, and truth? These are troublesome questions to   answer. However, if we are to move forward as a nation, it is essential that we come together and   remember the values that our founders fought for. Only then can we bridge the divide and form meaningful connections with one another, regardless of political affiliation. In order to answer these critical questions, we must take a step back and look at our nation's past.

By examining the values that our founders held dear and striving to embody them ourselves, we can create a unified future where everyone can benefit and thrive together.

The next couple of years could define the country for generations to come. We are at a crossroads, a new challenge facing our country. Will the norms up-date or will people continue to express anger and cruelty in public discourse? This is in part why I wrote this manifesto. I believe that Americans will value truth, despite that truth has been driven out of public sight. This is for manipulators to sell division, fear, and hate. Recent polls show that most Americans are in favor of immigration reform. However, media outlets still report it is a divisive issue. To counter the manipulators, I call for an end to anger and cruelty in public discourse. I also call to enforce updated norms that reflect the values of the majority. By doing so, we can restore truth and help to move away from the fear, division, and hate that have become all too common.

I hope this manifesto serves as a call to action for all Americans. This manifesto will raise awareness of the rampant partisan news and disinformation that is flooding   social media platforms. We need an independent press can provide fact-based truth. If our souls are in search of and pursuing happiness, then truth and facts should be an ideal we aspire to again, along with fairness and equality. Our souls should be free from the influences of hate and fear. We must act now to protect our society from the dangers of disinformation.

We also ensure that we have access to reliable news sources that are not beholden to any party or agenda. This is the only way to ensure that everyone has access to the truth, which is essential for a functioning democracy. driving force that started this country was independence. It was one of our country's guiding principles.

This is not just an American problem. It's an existential threat to democracy all around the globe. Without access to reliable news sources, it becomes impossible to make informed decisions for voting. If we allow news sources to be   influenced by political agendas, then we are allowing politicians to decide on our behalf. This defeats the purpose of having a democracy. To protect democracy and prevent uninformed decision-making, it is essential to ensure that political agendas do not influence news sources.

Issues

America's wounds are deep and inherited. We pass down injustices from generation to generation with no redemption. For this manifesto, I am focusing on reconciliation before redemption. I believe we can unite as a country and reconcile ourselves to our differences and injustices without demanding redemption. The concept of reconciliation before redemption is rooted   because we can come together and recognize our collective history without having to ask for forgiveness or make reparations. This approach allows us to move forward in a way that acknowledges our past without having to revisit it. By embracing this concept, we can heal the wounds of our past and create a more fair and just society for the future. As the famous American writer William Faulkner once wrote:
"The past is never dead. It's not even past."

The belief that groups have exclusive rights to their own histories is known as cultural appropriation. Once identity politics gains momentum, it subdivides, giving rise to ever-proliferating group identities demanding recognition. Nationwide, injustices should not be a cause for shame, but there needs to be justice before there can ever be redemption.

Transgressions are called out daily on social media; no one is immune. Cultural appropriation is an act of power in which members of dominant or majority groups adopt elements of a minority or oppressed culture without permission or understanding. This often results in the commodification of these elements, which leads to the trivialization and even erasure of the minority or oppressed culture. One group can impose its culture on another group without regard to the latter group's wishes, which they view as intellectual imperialism. As a result, it prevented oppressed cultures from expressing and preserving their own ethnic identity and customs. Early examples of cultural appropriation include white Westerners wearing cornrows and adopting music genres such as jazz or hip hop.

Political Polarization

Today's America is incapable of standing up for a country without identity politics. Political parties to push fear into all groups so they feel threatened, disrespected, or mistreated, so they will become defensive and retreat into tribalism. Identity politics allows political parties to manipulate and exploit the fears and insecurities of certain groups to gain power and influence. When people feel threatened, they are more likely to rally around a particular party or ideology, creating a sense of solidarity but fostering division. It becomes a fight between us and them because everyone else is to blame. Sadly, there is some truth behind these fears. Many groups face persecution and discrimination. It is tribal behavior that breeds bullying groups, such as itself or anyone who threatens the tribe. Social media and broadcast media play a vital role in dividing our society.

For instance, on certain platforms, they often pit people from different backgrounds against each other, and the resulting conversations can become hostile and divisive. This tribal mentality is driven by a fear of the "other", which is reinforced by the media and society, creating an "us vs. them" mentality. This leads to a lack of understanding and empathy between groups and creates an environment in which discrimination, bigotry, and hate can thrive. Therefore, it is imperative that we recognize the power of our words and use them to unite rather than divide.

Social media and some television networks contribute to polarizing people and intensifying animosity among groups in order to reinforce preconceived notions. They do this by presenting one-sided arguments and stories that inflame people's emotions and to get them to react in a certain way. This can lead to a further divide between people and an increase in hostility and animosity. This is more catastrophic than anything I've seen before. Both groups are pushing at each other. Each group accepts whatever false information the identity groups spread. Both sides can lie. Each trust's in partisan rhetoric with no regard to truth. This perpetuates a cycle of distrust and misunderstanding, making it harder for people to come together and find common ground. The lack of a shared understanding of facts can lead to an increase in polarization between the two sides. This makes it more difficult for them to find middle ground and resolutions. Watching capitalism and mass control through an abundance of media forms contributes to the issue. Someone knows every detail about you. Using technology, we can tailor deception to make you believe in untruths. This manipulation of facts, combined with the use of technology, can have profound consequences for our ability to come together and agree. It is paramount that we strive to foster an environment of trust and understanding, in order to make sure we are all on the same page.

Historical Reasons

America has faced many periods of intense disagreement and strife. Extreme populism has spread through various forms of   disinformation. Racial resentment has reached the highest levels. White fear is being promoted on social media. Fear that whites will no longer be the predominant group, forcing a tribal reaction. Racial animus is at a high rate right now. Other beliefs, like anti-intellectualism, are widespread in rural areas of America. Thus, giving rise to anti-rationalism. People prioritize emotions and beliefs over facts and reality, creating an atmosphere of distrust and paranoia. Leading to a situation where people are more likely to trust false information and conspiracy theories, which can lead to extreme and dangerous actions. This has created a sense of an "us vs them" mentality, where people of different backgrounds and beliefs are the enemy, leading to further division and xenophobia. A willingness to accept propaganda and wild ideas comes with populist culture. This is further compounded by the rise of social media, which gives people an easy way to spread misinformation and conspiracy theories with no sort of fact-checking. The lack of accountability makes it easy for people to accept these theories without question, and the echo chamber of like-minded people on social media only reinforces these beliefs.

Bad Actor Influence

Non-citizens attempting to spread propaganda and penetrate America's democracy is a genuine danger. A more pressing danger is that American citizens are not recognizing the threat.

It is imperative for American citizens to be aware of the potential for foreign entities to spread false information and manipulate public opinion. Unless citizens can recognize the threat, they're vulnerable to manipulation, resulting in inaccurate decisions that could have negative consequences.

Russia and China have been involved in attempting to influence our elections and add divisive rhetoric to the social media ethos. Such attempts can cause people to question the democratic. process, erode trust in public institutions, and create confusion and mistrust among citizens. If people are not aware of the threat and cannot recognize the signs of manipulation, they may be more likely to fall victim to such tactics, leading to inaccurate decisions and potential long-term consequences. This is true regardless of which side of the fence you are on. For the sake of this manifesto, it matters how you respond to this so you can avoid fake news propaganda in the future.

An educated public is essential in avoiding manipulation and fake news propaganda. That is because the more knowledge a person has, the better equipped they are to distinguish between accurate and false information. An informed public is more likely to recognize when they are being manipulated or lied to and can make more informed decisions. If both extremes are being manipulated, then the real enemy isn't the others. It's whoever is feeding you propaganda. They are doing it with bots and your personal information, a deadly combination. By manipulating both sides of a debate, they can create an atmosphere of confusion and distrust, where it's difficult to tell what is real and what is fake. This makes it easier for them to control the narrative and push their own agenda. In this way, true power lies not in the hands of those arguing, but in the hands of those behind the curtains, orchestrating the entire debate.

If both extremes are being manipulated, then the real enemy isn't the others. It's whoever is feeding you propaganda. They are doing it with bots and your personal information, a deadly combination. By manipulating both sides of a debate, they can create an atmosphere of confusion and distrust, where it's difficult to tell what is real and what is fake. This makes it easier for them to control the narrative and push their own agenda. In this way, true power lies not in the hands of those arguing, but in the hands of those behind the curtains, orchestrating the entire debate.

The R's and D's

In this section, I want to touch on problems or long-standing issues that take too long to cover in a manifesto. Recommending a disruptive action step for the future, I will shed light on the issue. Old ways have gotten America here. We need disruptive solutions to change the future. The old ways of doing things have not been wrong, but they have become outdated. We need to be open to trying novel approaches, even if they are disrupting, in order to create a better future. Disruptive solutions can be a positive force for change and progress. These solutions may require us to step out of our comfort zones, but that is often necessary to move forward. We need disruptive solutions to break free from the status quo and create a more fair and just future. These solutions can help us move beyond the limitations of the past and   create a more prosperous future. By embracing disruptive solutions, we can empower ourselves to make real and lasting change, while contributing to secure a more prosperous future for generations to come.

Refuge

America is a nation of immigrants. It should increase the number of immigrants every year, as emerging fields need experts and enthusiasts who can contribute to nation-building. It helps in promoting the economy of the nation. Immigrants with knowledge, skills, and dedication can benefit from this.

Several challenges faced by immigrants include unpredictable and lengthy case   processing timelines, to get their green cards and permanent residence. The U.S. Citizenship and Immigration Services (USCIS) is the federal agency responsible for processing these cases, and often backlogged because of a high volume of applications. This can lead to delays in processing, which can frustrate for immigrants who are waiting for their green cards and permanent residence.

Other nations hold America in reverence as being the only country in the world to accept and assimilate people from other nations, ethnicities, and cultures. The world comes here and reconciles itself to each other because of the American Dream. The American Dream stands as an example of hope and acceptance to the world, inspiring unity and togetherness amongst diverse people. Freedom is the beacon of hope that draws everyone here and we show the potential democracy shows the world for the future. America must decide what its attitude is going to be toward immigrants.

Action Steps: *Our understanding of immigrants must expand beyond stereotypes and disrupt the rhetoric of fear. We must embrace immigrants for the unique contributions and perspectives they bring to our society.*

*We must work to create a more welcoming environment for.
immigrants to ensure everyone can reach their full potential.*

Repentance

Although repentance has a religious connotation, to repent is to
change one's way of thinking and feeling in order to understand,
show remorse, and even to transform our thinking. Repentance,
also known as contrition, penitence, or remorse, is vital in having
the resolve to change. They needed this in a nation that has
wronged so many groups from women, indigenous peoples,
slaves and many others. Our nation has espoused from its
beginnings as a nation that we should provide equal
opportunities without a healthy amount of remorse.

There needs to be a certain amount of genuine regret, remorse,
as well as contrition, and commitment to actual action in order to
be saved as a nation. We mistreated and disenfranchised many
groups on our way to   becoming the beacon of freedom America
is today.

Action Steps: *We need to change old attitudes and learn the truth
about our past   injustices. We must commit to educating
ourselves and others to ensure a fairer and more fair future. This
requires us to confront the uncomfortable realities of our history
and to examine our own beliefs and biases. We must also work to
dismantle systemic racism and oppressive structures that have
been in place for centuries. Only then can we create an inclusive,
fair, and just society.*

Redemption

"When the architects of our republic wrote the magnificent words of the Constitution and the Declaration of Independence, they were signing a promissory note to which every American was to fall heir. This note was a promise that all men–yes, black men as well as white men would be guaranteed their unalienable rights of life, liberty, and the pursuit of happiness."
-Dr Martin Luther King Jr.

This is a much harder topic. Taking action to atone for past mistakes is no simple task to cover. Deliverance from the past is a burden on our nation. It hinders everyone from being equal in all ways. Understanding history can help keep us from repeating the mistakes of the past. The redemptive process gives us all a chance to come together in unity, contributing to the overall national good. Revelations of our past can unlock positive changes for our future.

Action Steps: *We must disrupt and take action to reclaim our history and provide solutions for those who are oppressed. We must take bold steps, challenging the status quo, and advocating for fairness, justice, and equity. By challenging the status quo and recognizing equality and justice, we can create a brighter future for everyone. This is the only way to ensure that they give all people the respect and opportunity they deserve.*

Restitution or Reparations?

We use our authority and power to seek justice, influence an injustice, or to restore something that is damaged. We must first reconcile if we want any type of unity. What will it take to re-unite the United States? Is each group's injustice more likely to be addressed if our nation is more united? It will take understanding the history of the country and a willingness to recognize the experiences of all groups. We must be open to hearing the stories of those who have been marginalized and work to address any injustices that we have committed. It is important to focus on the commonalities we all share and work to build bridges between different communities. A more unified nation will give us a better chance at addressing injustices and restoring unity. We must emphasize empathy and compassion, as well as education and understanding, in order to create a just and fair society.

Action Steps: *We need everyone to get involved. Pastors, ministers, rabbis, sages all should find disruptive ways of speaking empathy and compassion for our fellow man. Everyone has a unique platform and can use it to spread a message of love and understanding. People from all walks of life must come together and raise their voices for those who are marginalized and oppressed. As a result, we must all commit to do whatever we can to support and uplift those who are less fortunate and foster an environment of inclusiveness and respect. Together, we can create lasting, positive change.*

Reconciliation

Healing takes time. The first step in reconciliation is to understand that it will take time for our nation to heal from wounds that stem back hundreds of years. For instance, the ongoing protests against systemic racism have exposed the deep divisions and racial injustice that still exists in our society today. It will require ongoing effort from all parts of the country to work together, to be open and honest in dialogue, and to make meaningful changes. This process will be challenging, but if we all come together, it is possible to build a better future for all. The current systems that have been in place have been unsuccessful in addressing the issues facing people of color and other marginalized communities. Work together to create a new system that is built on equity and inclusion, and that values the diversity of our country.

Commit to this process and continue to build a society where everyone shows respect and dignity to each other. We accept this process will not be easy, but it is a necessary step towards achieving justice and equality for all.

There are fixable issues resulting from our identity. Instead of focusing on differences, consider similarities. If your identity as a father is strong, then look at others that have similarities with you as a father. Can America become more united? By finding commonalities and similarities among different people, we can create a more inclusive and tolerant society. When we can bridge the gaps between us, we can create more meaningful connections and strengthen our sense of unity. We can still form a strong bond despite our differences. By identifying and celebrating these   mutual connections, we can cultivate a sense of unity that can lead to a more united and tolerant society.

When we recognize and celebrate the commonalities among people, we can see past the differences. We can focus on our shared experiences and values, which can help us create a more understanding environment where everyone feels accepted and respected. By building a sense of community, we can create a more unified and tolerant society. It is possible to foster a culture of acceptance and cooperation by doing this.

Our values, experiences, and perspectives can create a more harmonious world. We can show appreciation for our differences and use them to build a more tolerant and fair environment. Through understanding, respect, and appreciation of each other, we can make a real difference in promoting unity and inclusivity. As a nation, we need to deepen our understanding of democracy. Americans won't be able to govern ourselves unless we figure out how to work with people we disagree with to solve genuine problems. This means that we need to move away from a polarized political landscape where compromise is a weakness. Instead, we need to move towards an environment where we value dialogue and collaboration. We need to understand how our democracy works so that we can work together to solve the issues facing our nation.

Starting at the local city level with organized public conversations about concrete issues would be a helpful start. It's almost impossible to have rational conversations about national topics like gun control in the wake of a mass shooting. By discussing issues at a local, grassroots level, more people will be engaged in the conversation. We can develop solutions on a smaller scale before implementing them. If successful, we can replicate these solutions on a larger scale.

Creating an environment of rational dialogue at the grassroots level is essential to the success of any national conversation.

Allowing this facilitates a more comprehensive understanding of the issue and enables more successful solutions to be developed. I think we could develop stronger models of democracy at the city level, following our founder's intention for us to have a deliberate democracy.

The hope for Americans is in the promise of democracy to bring people of different cultures and viewpoints together. They will work for a larger common good. We could achieve this by giving local governments more autonomy to create laws and policies that reflect the needs of their citizens, while also allowing citizens to have more input into the decision-making process. This would create a stronger model of democracy that reflects the values of our founders and ensures that we met the needs of citizens. The right to self-determination is fundamental to the American democratic system. For example, local governments could pass laws that give citizens the right to vote on issues that affect their lives, such as housing, transportation, and education.

I have focused this manifesto on our commonalities and on a path to reconciliation. Commonalities such as the American Dream and the spirit of entrepreneurship! By emphasizing these shared values and goals, we can create a sense of unity and understanding. This is essential in order to build bridges and find a way forward together. It is the only way we can achieve reconciliation and a better future for all. The American Dream and the spirit of entrepreneurship are pathways that can bring us together, build bridges, and foster reconciliation. Through these shared values and goals, we can create unity, understanding and a brighter future for us all.

Action Steps: *We must disrupt and become reconcilers, bringing people together in unity.*

By focusing on the common elements of the American Dream and Entrepreneurship, we can create an atmosphere of collaboration, cooperation and understanding. We can use these values to bridge divides and develop a stronger, more prosperous society. We must seek opportunities to engage, build relationships and foster dialogue among different people. By taking small steps, we can create a more united, fair world.

Disruption

"We have all come on different ships,
but we're all on the same boat now."
-Dr. Martin Luther King Jr.

Make no mistake, America is in an existential fight for democracy. America is a country with a flawed start but with massive potential. Abraham Lincoln mentioned in the Gettysburg Address how we are a nation "conceived in liberty" and dedicated to the proposition that he created all men. It is now up to us to take up that fight and help America realize the dream it can achieve. We can do this by reshaping our understanding and letting go of the red and blue labels and putting the country first.

Americans are thirsty to get past this balance between civility and nastiness, hope and hate, and truth and lies. By coming together, we can bridge the gap between   different beliefs and opinions and create a more unified America where we respect every individual and give them the opportunity to succeed. We need to create an environment that embraces diversity and brings out the best in everyone. With this, we can create an America that realizes the promise of the Gettysburg Address and works towards building a brighter future for all.

To achieve this, we must come together as a nation and recognize that our unity strengthens us than our division. We must also recognize that we are all members of one community and that we all have something to contribute to the common good. Only then will we reach our fullest potential as a nation.

As voters, we must demand more from our politicians (representatives) and force them to represent the people before their parties. We must find our voice and increase the number of voters that take part. It's up to the people to take back the country and look for solutions outside of the political realm. This is by reclaiming back power for the people and forcing the parties to represent their constituents.

It's time to disrupt politics like we disrupt business. Let's find original solutions to the problems that face our nation. The old ways haven't worked. It's only given power to a two-party system that has failed us.

This is who we are. In the aftermath of a partisan war, a tribe faced two tough choices: Choosing a future where a civil war loomed or choosing to reaffirm allegiance to the country.

It's why we used to recite the pledge at school every day. Pledging allegiance to the country first, we can come together to bridge the divide between the two tribes.

This will enable us to create a future that works for everyone. This will require people to recognize compromise and to put their partisan beliefs aside in order to work together for the greater good.

The Pledge

"I pledge allegiance to the flag of the United States of America and to the Republic for which it stands, one nation, under God, indivisible with liberty and justice for all."

Action Steps: We demand, disrupt, and pledge to save America and democracy together because we feel compelled to do so. It is our duty as citizens to protect our democracy and the freedoms that come with it. We must take action to hold our elected officials accountable and to ensure that we run our country in a manner that is beneficial to all. We must demand justice, disrupt the status quo, and work together for our nation. As citizens, it is our responsibility to take a stand and ensure that it does not take our democracy for granted. We must use our collective power to create meaningful change and promote a fair society where everyone respects and dignifies each other. By pledging our commitment to these values, we can ensure that America and democracy remain strong and vibrant.

#demandanddisrupt #savedemocracy #saveamerica

"That dream of a land in which life should be better and richer
and fuller for every man, with opportunity for each
according to his ability or achievement."
-James Truslow Adams, The Epic of America 1931

The American Dream

The original American dream was not about individual wealth.
It was a dream of equality, justice and democracy for the nation.
Each generation has repurposed the concept until it became a
consumer capitalist version of democracy. This has corrupted the
core idea of the American Dream to prioritize individual success
and wealth over collective success. As a result, it has become a
dream of material prosperity instead of a dream of a just and fair
society. This has resulted in a skewed interpretation of the
American Dream, where the emphasis is on individual gain
rather than on collective progress and the common good.

Capitalism ideology's version of the American dream contains a
belief that competitive behavior is natural. A suggestion that
human beings compete and will therefore try to gain many
things. Combining this idea with Charles Darwin's idea of "survival
of the fittest" has produced a morphed view of the dream that
only the strong can achieve. This ideology suggests that success
is only possible through competition. It also assumes that those
who are most successful are the most competitive, and that they
are the ones who will end up with the best outcome. This
competitive mindset implies that those who don't compete
cannot achieve the American dream.

Those who don't have the same resources may be at a disadvantage and find it difficult to achieve the American dream. For instance, the emphasis on competition may lead to the idea that those from lower socio-economic backgrounds have less of an opportunity to succeed, regardless of their hard work and dedication. This competitive mindset is like a race the more resources you have, the further ahead you are. Those with fewer resources may find it hard to compete and keep up and are thus at a disadvantage. The word "competition" derives from the Latin verb competere, which means "to meet, come together."

Competition often involves two or more individuals or teams coming together in some kind of contest. Competition can be a powerful motivator, but it can also lead to unhealthy comparisons and feelings of inadequacy. It is important to remember that competition should always be positive, focused on personal growth and improvement. We should always view competition as a chance to better oneself and strive for growth, rather than who is "better" than the other person.

The American Dream as an ideal is that everybody, no matter where they come from, has equal access to opportunities if they work hard for it. We root our philosophy in the American ideals of democracy. Equate American system of capitalism allows everyone to fulfill their dreams because of its principles of equality, rights, liberty, and opportunity. Americans believe in their own version of the dream. Each has their own definition of happiness, love, and money.

Excerpt from: "The Pursuit" Podcast with Tel Ganesan

"What is it about entrepreneurs that's different from the rest of us? Entrepreneurs compete because of the passion and drive in their belly. The American dream changes but we keep pursuing it. The journey is the American dream. It's the pursuit of something, making a change. Entrepreneurs have a unique set of skills and traits that set them apart from the rest of us. We motivate them to pursue their dreams despite the inherent risk and uncertainty. Risks to make their dreams a reality, and they have the courage and resilience to persevere even when the odds are against them. They are also resourceful, finding new ways to solve problems and overcome obstacles. They have an unwavering commitment to their vision, and the   dedication to see it through to the end."

America is the land of entrepreneurs. They are the people who founded this country, so to me, pursuing entrepreneurship is pursuing the American dream. We are all the same. Maybe it's time for humanity to reset itself and treat everybody the same and follow this journey of humanity. You must raise your awareness level. Whatever you do, you must do it with intention, and do it with passion and focus.

Give 100% to whatever you do. Entrepreneurship is a way to create opportunities, to build something from nothing, and to bring positive change to the world. It is also a way to gain financial freedom and to live on one's own terms. The idea of pursuing the American Dream is part of the spirit of the country. It can inspire people to work hard and strive for greatness. Incorporating intention, passion, and focus, entrepreneurs can take advantage of the American Dream to build something meaningful and gain financial freedom. Entrepreneurship is the cornerstone of what has made this country so successful. The only way to achieve true financial freedom and security, and it allows people to pursue their passions and ideas. A way to matter in the world and create something that will last long after we're gone. It is not enough to have an idea or a plan you must put in the work to make it happen. Successful entrepreneurs understand that any goal worth achieving requires dedication and sacrifice, but in the end, it is worth it for the satisfaction and success it brings.

Despite being the 11th wealthiest nation and having access to almost 25% of the world's resources, the happiness index is dipping. According to the World Health Organization, one out of five people has some degree of mental illness, and most often depression. What can we do better? How can we better our lives? We designed the current economic and social systems to prioritize capital over people, which creates an environment of competition and stress that can lead to dissatisfaction. We need to create a society where people prioritize relationships, empathy, and community over money and materialism. This shift to a more holistic and sustainable lifestyle will lead to improved mental health and overall well-being. To create a fair and. satisfying society, we must shift our focus away from acquiring material wealth and towards valuing relationships, empathy, and community.

To resolve these issues, I draw on my Eastern roots. Traditional Eastern practices such as meditation and mindfulness. These practices can help us become more aware of our thoughts and feelings, allowing us to gain control over them. It can help us better regulate our emotions, which can reduce the symptoms of depression. Mindfulness and meditation can help to improve our relationships with others, which can be   beneficial for overall mental health. The sense of community and connection that is often found in Eastern cultures can provide valuable support to those suffering from mental illness. Not only this, but mindfulness and meditation can be a great way to process difficult emotions, as well as cultivate a sense of inner peace and harmony.

1. **Values:** Ideologies like trust, friendliness, and mutual respect are important both for an individual and the organization. As the coordination among the team members raises, there would be a common focus to support their team members and win as a team. I have learned it throughout trial and error, having been the aggressive leader at one point and the bored team member at another. Learning does not come overnight. They advised me to stay awake and seek the yogi's sense of balance, which can instill a deep calmness even though it requires intense and unwavering alertness. This means that each team member must maintain a sense of awareness of the goals, progress, and issues of the group. Everyone must support each other and focus on the team's effort, instead of individual achievement. Doing this will motivate and unify the team, equipping them better to reach their goals.

2. **Empowerment:** Empowerment is the art of serendipity. People in all walks of life need permission to fail sometimes. Failure is the only way to discover something new and unpredictable. It also empowers them to do their best and to see beyond the norm.

Common sense would have had me stick to information technology as the prime way to keep my business going through any economic cycle. People can take risks to generate innovative ideas and solutions that they haven't thought of. This allows them to develop their skills and grow. It allows them to think of creative solutions that they had not considered before. By taking the risk of investing in a diverse range of areas, I have been able to secure financial stability and maximize my potential for growth. I had studied the process, worked in it for 20 years, and hired capable people to conduct business in the USA and India. But I wanted an additional risk. As an Indian movie maker, Bollywood became a worldwide phenomenon. I produced several movies in America with the help of Indian technology. I also added business streams in the health and wellness market, and published magazines.

3. **Excellence:** Excellence is a value that is being prized in any business or life situation. In my company, we say the best of the best. The world requires only the best of the best. I believe that excellence is perfection. Strive for incremental improvement, which is the key to becoming a creative genius in your field of enterprise. When you feel as though you have mastered your craft, try even harder, as life is a journey. By striving for excellence, you are pushing yourself to do better and to be better. With incremental improvement, you can find creative ways to solve problems and find success in any endeavor. Excellence is not only perfection, but it is also a mindset of never settling and never giving up. It is about setting high standards for yourself and striving to achieve them. People can practice and achieve excellence with consistency and determination. It is pushing yourself to go further, to move beyond the limits of what you know and do, in order to reach the next level of success.

4. **Passion:** Passion is a positive and inspiring force, and when maneuvering, it becomes one of the inherent forces of motivation. We have a process called follow up to follow up. We check in with people often to see how they relate to their assignments and how they complete them. It is a leader's job to convey excitement or find another placement where this same person might thrive. In a big company, there are multiple opportunities. If you give up and judge, you might miss that chance of utilizing an outstanding talent. Following up is important to ensure that everyone agrees with their assignments, as well as to understand how well they are performing. It also gives leaders the opportunity to redirect individuals if they aren't succeeding in their current role, to ensure that their talents are being used in the best way possible. By staying alert and communicating, you can make the most of the opportunities within a large company and better use the talents of the individuals involved.

5. **Happiness:** We build our entire life's purpose on happiness, whether in work, home, or in the community we live in. When you find it in one sector, you can find it almost anywhere. I try to encourage those who are unhappy to ease up on self-criticism. The fear of doing something wrong might stop someone from embarking on the first step, let alone completing it. In the recovery community, the most repeated phrase is, let God. Believe a spiritual force can help you when you tremble and can help you regain your strengths. This phrase encourages us to surrender to something higher than ourselves and to trust that what we are doing is the right thing. It helps us to take risks, to move forward, and to believe in ourselves. It also helps us to accept failure and to forgive ourselves when we make mistakes. Emphasizing this concept, we must remember to act, but also to trust in a higher power to guide us along the way.

The Declaration of Independence defines the pursuit of happiness as a fundamental right, allowing people to pursue joy and love life in a way that makes them happy, provided they do nothing illegal or violate the rights of others. The Declaration of Independence states all people have the right to life, liberty, and the pursuit of happiness, and that governments should not interfere with that right. It guarantees that people have the freedom to pursue their own goals and dreams on condition that they do not infringe on the rights of others. The Declaration of Independence serves as a reminder that governments should not stand in the way of individuals seeking to pursue their goals and make their lives better.

The ideal of freedom is to be free. An individual's well-being depends on this. The law shall afford no class of people less protection than that enjoyed by other groups and individuals in their lives, liberty, property, and pursuit of happiness.

America is engaged in a long-term fight for democracy and the question is: can democracy survive in the digital era? The 2024 Presidential election is going to be an actual battle for the soul of the country. Citizens will we be partisan patrons of hate or united citizens behind the hope of the Americans' dream and the kindness of its people to care for their fellow man. Securing the attention span of the public may be the determinator of the country's survival.

This fight is not just about political ideologies, but also the ability to reach people and make them understand how important the upcoming election is. The digital era has made it easier to spread false information, with social media and other platforms, which has made it more difficult to control the narrative. It is the citizens responsibility and research the facts to make sure it informed them before they cast their vote.

Emphasizing the importance of the upcoming election, it is crucial for citizens to take the time to research and verify the facts before making their decision, as the digital age has made it easier for false information to spread. Part of the attractiveness for immigrants to come to America is often because there is more freedom to become rich or successful than the country that they are leaving.

The American Dream has been a long-time model of prosperity for both Americans and people around the world. Expected success has brought millions of immigrants to America, charming them into looking for equal opportunity and a better life. For many immigrants, the idea of the American Dream provides them with a sense of hope and a possibility that they might not have had in their home country. With the promise of a better life immigrants can take advantage of the opportunities available to them in the United States, such as access to education, employment, and economic security. Immigrants are driven by their dreams of success, and the opportunities that the United States can offer them to make those dreams a reality is an invaluable motivator. With the right support and resources, they can achieve the American Dream and build a better future for themselves and their families.

Standard icons of the American Dream are a beacon to the world that there is hope for a future. Icons such as democracy, equal rights, and freedom, giving everyone an equal chance to succeed. Regardless of where, or what class, they were born into, anyone can attain their own version of success and upward mobility. They achieved it through sacrifice, and hard work, not by chance.

For example, many immigrants to the United States have attained the American Dream through their hard work, dedication, and resilience in the face of adversity.

Excerpt from "The Pursuit" Podcast with Tel Ganesan

"The American dream keeps changing. We keep pursuing; the journey is the American dream. It's the pursuit of something, and making a change. You want to shape your passion and drive. America is the land of entrepreneurs. They founded this country that way and, to me, pursuing entrepreneurship is pursuing the American dream. We are all the same. Maybe it's time for humanity to reset itself and treat everybody the same and follow this journey the humanity journey. This is because the American dream has become more about individual achievement than collective success, and people want to use their own skills, creativity, and ambition to achieve their goals and impact the world. It has become more about pursuing something   meaningful, rather than pursuing material wealth. Today's American Dream is being able to graduate from college with minimal debt. Secure a job in your field that has benefits, be able to afford health care costs, while saving for retirement and paying down loans, and still live a comfortable life.

This means that everyone should have the same opportunity to access quality education, pursue their career goals, and live a life of comfort and security. We must strive to make this American Dream a reality for all."

It is still possible to achieve the American Dream, but it has taken on a unique form in the modern world. We now often measure success by an individual's level of job satisfaction, sense of purpose, and overall quality of life, rather than financial success. The American Dream is now more about achieving a sense of financial security, freedom, and autonomy, as opposed to the traditional concept of owning a house and having a successful career. That said, it is still possible to achieve financial success and security with the right mindset and determination. With hard work, dedication, and a strong support system, it is still possible to achieve the modern American Dream.

The Global Millionaire Magazine Cover August 2022

"The founders of America with the Declaration of Independence
had the foresight with these three tenants,
"Life, Liberty and the Pursuit of happiness",
you can have all the material things in the world but, if
you are not happy it means nothing without happiness."
-Tel Ganesan
Serial Entrepreneur and Global Humanitarian

Entrepreneurship

The United States is the most entrepreneurial nation on planet earth. Benjamin Franklin was one of the first entrepreneurs in the United States. According to Archibald Marwizi, "Entrepreneurship is discovering creative ways of combining resources to create change in whatever area of life."

I am optimistic that we can disrupt the current problems that the country faces by creating and developing a younger generation of innovative entrepreneurs. Political and macroeconomic conditions are favorable for America's future. It has withstood the test of time will continue to do so.

America has reinvented itself will continue to lead innovation and entrepreneurs will lead the way with their contributions to society. For instance, the current pandemic has created the need for unprecedented technological innovation, and many entrepreneurs have stepped up to the challenge by creating new products and services to address the issue.

The relationship between entrepreneurship and economic development is important to understand. The benefits and drawbacks of entrepreneurship, if handled correctly, can cause a positive economic and societal impact.

Entrepreneurs create jobs, which stimulate economic growth and development. They can bring new products and services to the market, which can increase competition and reduce prices. This can lead to higher quality and more affordable products, which is beneficial to both producers and consumers. Entrepreneurship can create opportunities for people who may have been excluded or marginalized.

This is especially true in developing countries, where most of the population is unemployed and there is a lack of access to basic services. By creating new jobs, entrepreneurs can help to reduce poverty, increase incomes, and improve living standards. They can bring new skills and technologies to the market, which can help to spur economic growth and development. We can therefore see entrepreneurship as a powerful tool for tackling economic inequality, providing opportunity and economic security to many who would otherwise go without.

Excerpt from "The Pursuit" Podcast with Tel Ganesan

"If you didn't start early on, there's plenty of time to . become an entrepreneur. From tech entrepreneurship, films, fashions, and wellness, I've done everything under the sun. I think the best place to start is interning with companies, and start networking, going to conferences, join various clubs and get to know people. A lot of things in the entrepreneurial world are about action. It's not theory. Entrepreneurship is hands on. Taking the initiative and following through on your ideas is key to entrepreneur-ship. Taking initiative and following through on your ideas is not only key to success, it is also the defining factor of an entrepre-neur. There will always be something new to discover and imple-ment, so it is important to be open to learning. Building relation-ships and making connections are important resources. Take the time to research and plan, as this will help you figure out the best way to move forward with your business. Entrepreneurship requires you to be both proactive and open-minded, using the relationships and resources you have to inform your decisions and plan out your next steps. You should find a mentor that can give you knowledge that you can apply. This is where you can make progress. I have done this on my journey, creating larger ecosystems from the city, county, and state levels. This helps you to identify key stakeholders that can help you scale your business and hone your ideas.

Having a mentor can also be essential in helping you to navigate the complexities of setting up a business, as they can provide valuable insight into the processes and decisions that need to be made. Taking this further, having a mentor to assist you with the intricacies of business operations, such as understanding and. adhering to relevant regulations, can be crucial in ensuring the long-term success of any venture."

Disruptive Thinking

Entrepreneurs are free thinkers. Natural creative disruptors. Small businesses and business owners thrive on learning and adapting, which requires fresh thinking, new ideas and unusual approaches to problem solving. Needs or concerns from consumers are more easily picked up on by small business owners, hence they are more likely to understand. Entrepreneurs often possess the capacity for disruptive thinking, which involves questioning traditional assumptions, taking risks, and trying fresh approaches to the status quo. Disruptive thinking enables entrepreneurs to push boundaries and find new solutions to existing problems. For instance, a small business owner might spot a new trend in the market and create a product to meet that need, whereas a larger business might not have the ability to develop a new product. By embracing disruptive thinking, entrepreneurs can identify opportunities that larger businesses may not can pursue and use this to their advantage.

Starting businesses or selling products and services generates paychecks that entrepreneurs can invest in local communities. I want to see a fresh wave of entrepreneurs that thrive and prioritize building up their local communities and support schools, clubs, charities, and organizations.

Generating funds to help solve problems and generating more consumers at the same time. This can have an enormous positive impact on local communities, as these entrepreneurs can create jobs, provide economic stability, and encourage further investment in the area. Their profits can reinvest in the community, providing further economic and social benefits. For instance, a community-owned wind farm in a rural area can bring in renewable energy, jobs, and income to the local community, and can also be a source of pride. This can have an enormous positive impact, not only on local economies but also on individuals and families who, with improved quality of life and opportunities for growth. The profits from these businesses can reinvest in the community, bringing about further economic and social benefits for its citizens.

Social Entrepreneurs

Much of my mission is to create social entrepreneurs. Ones who can recognize a social problem and use entrepreneurial principles to manage, create, and organize ventures that can drive social change. They can recognize social challenges while using business solutions to solve them. A social entrepreneur is someone who uses business principles to identify, create, and manage ventures that address social challenges.

They combine creativity and innovation and understanding of social issues to create solutions that benefit both the community and the business. Social entrepreneurs strive to find creative solutions to problems that benefit both the business and the community. They recognize the need to balance the interests of both parties, and they understand that the success of a venture depends on both the financial and social benefits it can provide.

By taking a holistic approach to their work, social entrepreneurs have the potential to make a lasting impact that improves society and the environment, while also achieving financial returns.

Serving markets with new products for financial gain, while matching the business to social or environmental goals. Social ventures are not the same as charities. It is businesses with social objectives along with leaders that are risk takers. They can lead ventures with strong will power and creative innovation. Leaders create companies that emphasize social responsibility and provide solutions to social problems. Creative with an obvious purpose. They are strong enough and willing to reinvest profits back into the community. For instance, Warby Parker, an American online retailer of eyeglasses, donates a pair of glasses to someone in need for every pair bought, creating a sustainable business model that has a positive social impact.   Warby Parker is just one example of a responsible company. Other companies, such as Patagonia and Toms, have also shown their commitment to social responsibility by donating money to charitable causes, using sustainable materials, and offering employee benefits that support their communities. Taking it a step further, these companies have also implemented policies that encourage their customers to have positive effects on the environment, such as offering discounts for customers who recycle their products.

Imagine being able to create, promote and enhance local "ecosystems" with a clear aim to make communities better. Excellent at business and even better at serving humanity. In these ecosystems, we brought together the entrepreneurs and matched them with potential capital investors and corporate leaders that can help them grow the businesses. Such an approach would have many benefits. It would not only create more economic opportunities for local entrepreneurs but would also enable them to become more financially secure, create jobs and make the local community more vibrant. Also provided would be access to capital and expertise to help them scale their businesses and grow. Enabling local businesses to contribute to the region's overall economic development and bring in much needed revenue. I have done that for businesses and achieved at a large scale.

Now I'm looking to combine the business and the social components which, as a byproduct, will lead to more unity. I'm interested in fostering social entrepreneurs' interest in wellness, healthy living, environmental sustainability, improvement of individual communities, along with economic, gender and racial equality.

Excerpt from "The Pursuit" Podcast with Tel Ganesan

"I can think of two actions to take. Number one at the education level, and action number two. Once they leave college, we have to take the action that will spur real economic growth that will expand the economy. At the education level, we need to ensure that students are graduating with the skills and knowledge they need in the job market. Then, once they leave college, we need to create incentives and opportunities for them to use those skills and get jobs that offer living wages and benefits. This will create more jobs, grow the economy, and help

people achieve financial stability. We must invest in our future workforce by investing in quality education and meaningful employment opportunities. We need to focus more on entrepreneurship, as well as risk taking and decision making. These are economy changing and life altering education that will help people, communities, and the country. Investing in education will not only help people gain the knowledge and skills needed to succeed in the workplace, but it will also help to create an educated workforce who can contribute to the economic growth of the country. Focusing on entrepreneurship and risk taking will encourage innovation and creativity, which are essential components for a strong and sustainable economy. Investing in education and encouraging entrepreneurship and risk taking can be a powerful combination to foster economic prosperity by creating an educated workforce that is innovative and creative."

Innovation

Entrepreneurs create products and services that solve problems in innovative ways. Businesses must earn profits to survive. Entrepreneurs don't have the luxury of being impractical.

Their products and services must be functional, and they must be cost-effective and to appeal to enough people to make it practical to produce the products. Innovation is an important part of entrepreneurship. Entrepreneurs must be able to identify problems and develop creative solutions to address those problems.

They must also be able to identify new markets and create products and services that meet the needs of those markets.

For instance, the sharing economy has enabled development of new products and services that have disrupted traditional business models, such as Uber and Airbnb. By taking a creative approach to problem solving and exploring new markets entrepreneurs can develop successful business strategies that capitalize on disruptive opportunities.

Entrepreneurs adapted computers into a form that had widespread appeal and   practicality. Governments may mandate environmental standards that force individuals and businesses to reach a threshold level of sustainability. Entrepreneurs introducing products that are appealing and offer real world environmental solutions, their ideas get more traction. This is because when governments set standards, it creates a market for products that meet the requirements, and entrepreneurs are more likely to fill that market need if there is an opportunity to make a profit. As a   result, the incentive to create more sustainable solutions is more likely to be found in the private sector than in public policy alone.

Foundations and fundamentals continue to foster a robust business climate and   create avenues for continual innovation. Businesses stand to gain from being early adopters of sustainable solutions, as it can often lead to increased profits and customer loyalty. The private sector also has an advantage over government policy in that it can respond to the latest trends and technologies and change stay competitive. By staying ahead of the curve, businesses gain the advantage of being able to capitalize on new opportunities, while also staying abreast of the latest developments in the market. Furthermore, sustainable practices and solutions can lead to cost savings and greater customer loyalty. Embracing the fundamentals and foundations of business can help to ensure a business's long-term success.

Excerpt from "The Pursuit" Podcast with Tel Ganesan

"Let me break it down. Even within the US itself, there are a lot of differences from coast to coast. If you look at the mid-west, the culture or tolerance for risk or entrepreneurship, differs from in Silicon Valley. You might see a difference in Boston, and even more so when you go down south. Here in the Midwest, there is a conservative culture of taking risks. Midwesterners still like to get a nine-to-five job, so what we need to do is get entrepreneurship embedded into education and start promoting entrepreneurship. In the years to come, it's going to be a mainstream career. Because of the pandemic, we now have a lot of freelancers, so we might see entrepreneurship taking over from traditional careers. We can see taking risks to increase economic growth, which is why it's important to promote entrepreneurship by embedding it into education. The pandemic has caused a shift in the job market, with more people becoming freelancers, so there is an increased demand for entrepreneurship and the need to make it a mainstream career."

I'd Like to Meet

In Business it would honor me to meet Elon Musk. He's the only person in history that has taken knowledge in one industry and transported into other industries that are not similar. His investment into PayPal led to his birthing Tesla, and that has propelled him into the galaxies of space. There is no one that has started in the Financial Services Industry, then moved into the automotive industry and is now in the realm of space and space Travel. His success has been a remarkable journey, and it would inspire to hear how he has achieved such levels of greatness. For instance, his vision of revolutionizing the auto industry with sustainable energy has led him to launch his Tesla Roadster into space, with the goal of having a sustainable human presence on Mars.

In VC Funding I would like to meet Mark Cuban. I like his approach to investments and funding, and I also like his energy.

I believe his insight would be invaluable in helping my business secure the venture capital. Meeting Mark Cuban would be an incredible opportunity to gain valuable insight into the realm of venture capital fundraising and to benefit from his enthusiasm and energy.

In Sports, it would be fantastic to meet LeBron James. I like his mindset; he is a big believer in the mind's power. And he applies it to the way he approach's his sport. I too believe I can also apply the power of mind to my business. For instance, LeBron James uses visualization techniques to practice his game and I can use similar techniques to practice my business strategies.

Visualizing success is a key part of LeBron James' approach to sports, and I believe that we can also apply it to business to bring about similar results.

I believe if I have time to meet any of the individuals mentioned above, it will transform me into a higher level of consciousness. By listening to and interacting with individuals who have achieved a higher level of consciousness, it will expose me to new perspectives and ways of thinking that I wouldn't otherwise have access to. This could help me expand my understanding of the world and better equip me to reach greater levels of enlightenment.

To me, pursuing entrepreneurship is pursuing the American dream. Being an entrepreneur is not only an opportunity to create a successful business but also to make my dreams of achieving a higher level of success a reality. The entrepreneurial spirit is part of the American identity, and being able to take control of one's destiny by creating a successful business is. something that many people aspire to. Entrepreneurship offers the potential for greater financial reward, and the chance to use one's creativity and initiative to make their dreams come true. Entrepreneurs and social entrepreneurs need to have passion and drive in your belly if you want to matter. The American dream keeps changing as we change, but we keep pursuing. Pursuing the American dream is a key motivation for many entrepreneurs. It is the promise of a better life for ourselves and our families, and the opportunity to build something that will last for generations. The journey is the American dream. We are all the same. Maybe it's time for humanity to reset itself and treat everybody the same.

"You can never have an impact on society
if you have not changed yourself."
-Nelson Mandela

Algorithms

We live in a world where content is abundant and too much to consume. Algorithms play a crucial role in making sense of all this content. Algorithms can sort, filter, and recommend content that is tailored to a user's interests. This makes it easier to find the content that is most relevant, instead of having to search through all the content. Algorithms are not only useful in organizing content, but they also enable users to get content that is tailored to their individual needs and interests. This makes it more efficient for users to access the content they seek, without having to research and filtering.

However, algorithms can also have unintended consequences, such as forming filter bubbles, perpetuating bias, and restricting our choices and creativity. Often, Algorithms are based on past data, which can lead to them forming homogeneous digital spaces where people only interact with people like them and can lead to bias, as they can perpetuate existing stereotypes and inequality. Algorithms can limit our choices and creativity by presenting us with only a few options, instead of allowing us to explore other possibilities. As a result, algorithms can restrict our freedom of expression and limit our ability to express our creativity.

Many studies have shown that algorithms can trigger huge financial losses, promote unfair decisions, violate laws, and even cause deaths because of poor design, unintentional bias, or malicious interventions. They built algorithms on data that is often incomplete or biased. This means that the decisions made by the algorithms are not always accurate and can lead to unintended consequences. Malicious actors can also intervene and manipulate algorithms for their own gain, leading to even further losses and damage. We must create and maintain algorithms with a keen eye to accuracy, fairness, and security to combat this and ensure that they remain reliable and decide with the best possible outcomes. The currency of social media is our attention. Social media platforms use algorithms to capture our attention and make us stay online for longer. They also use targeted ads and other strategies to keep us   engaged and coming back for more. Our attention is valuable and needs to be respected. We should be cautious about what we allow ourselves to be exposed to online and make sure we don't get caught in a cycle of digital addiction. For instance, setting time limits for ourselves for using social media can be a good way to ensure we don't become too entrenched in digital consumption.

Social media algorithms serve up content based on what you've already interacted with, which can create a "rabbit hole" effect if left unchecked. Limiting time we spend on social media can help us avoid this "rabbit hole" effect by ensuring that we don't get too immersed in the content. This can also help us keep a   balanced lifestyle and avoid potential feelings of anxiety or depression that can arise from too much time spent online.

As you click, you can become exposed to an endless stream of content that may   become more niche or extreme. It is essential to be mindful of what content you are consuming and its potential impact on you.

We can create mass psychosis with social media because attention is its currency. They designed social media algorithms to keep users engaged on the platforms for long periods of time, which makes it easier to manipulate people with false information. This can lead to a collective psychosis, where large numbers of people believe things that aren't true. This can have a damaging effect on society, causing people to make poor decisions based on false beliefs and eroding faith in legitimate sources of information.

Computers are not required to do them. We are running algorithms in our brains.   Algorithms enable us to identify patterns and relationships in data, whether it be numbers, words, or images. By understanding these patterns, we can decide. We can save time and energy by using algorithms to find the best solution to a problem. Therefore, algorithms are essential tools for making sense of the world and helping us to make effective decisions.

An algorithm works as a shortcut for solving problems. By using an algorithm, it is possible to make quick and accurate decisions without having to delve into the specifics of the problem. Together, let's change the algorithms and create a massive social impact. Let's use our expertise in algorithms to drive meaningful and positive change for society.

"Human kindness has never weakened the stamina,
or softened the fiber of a free people.
A nation does not have to be cruel to be tough."
-Franklin D. Roosevelt
-32nd President of the United States of America

Social Impact

Social impact means any significant or positive changes that solve or at least addresses societal injustices and challenges. Businesses or organizations achieve these goals through conscious efforts or activities in their operations and administrations. Businesses or organizations provide affects to their consumers and the public all the time, though in different capacities. Social impact, however, is based on the direct positive consequences these parties offer to society. Social impact involves making intentional, positive changes to benefit a certain group of people, a certain community, or the entire world. It is not just about making profits, but also about leaving a lasting and sustainable impact on the world. Social impact involves not only providing resources and services to those in need but also creating meaningful and lasting change through education advocacy, and other forms of activism. It is not just about making money, but also about creating a better society and a better future for everyone. By making a lasting social impact, businesses can go   beyond making a profit and ensure that they felt the benefits across the board. For instance, a company could create a scholarship program to subsidize students from underprivileged backgrounds to pursue higher education or launch a campaign to raise awareness about a social issue.

Social impact comes from many sectors and industries. Public, private, plural, and fourth sectors all contribute differently to society. These sectors choose to operate with specific sets of goals and approaches to create significant social change. The public sector comprises government programs, while they made the private sector up of corporations. The plural sector comprises non-profits and NGOs, and the fourth sector comprises social enterprises. Each sector has different resources and capabilities to help create social change.

While each sector has its own distinct set of advantages, they all have one important thing in common; they all strive to create positive social change. As Harry Browne, an American libertarian author, once wrote: "You can't give the government the power to do good without also giving it the power to do bad, in fact, to do anything it wants."

Social impact began as a philanthropic effort to help those in need. Philanthropy is not something new. People and organizations have always been ready to lend a   helping hand since time began. Creating massive social change is my passion. I believe everyone can make changes that matter. Social impact is about creating   sustainable and long-lasting solutions to problems. It is about creating systems and structures that can benefit those in need and ensure that they met their needs in the long-term. It is about recognizing that it takes more than just a onetime donation to create genuine change.

To create social impact, we need to move beyond short-term solutions and look for long-term solutions that can bring lasting changes to those in need.

New Type of Empathy

"The level of our success is limited only by our imagination, and no act of kindness is ever wasted
-Aseop

To help achieve Social Impact Goals, I have fostered partnerships with global organizations that have successful programs in place. The United Nations created 17 Social Development Goals (SDGs) as a guide for organizations, businesses and individuals to create and develop significant social impact in the world. Aligning with successful organizations will help foster success and give us tremendous resources to learn from. For instance, I partnered with an organization that has a successful program in place to reduce poverty in the developing world. Through this partnership, I could access resources and insights to help develop our own program to reduce poverty. By partnering with a successful organization, we can take advantage of their knowledge and resources to help us achieve our goals. We can learn from their success stories and mistakes, which can help us develop a more effective program. Being associated with a successful organization will give us more credibility and access to resources that we may not have had access to otherwise.

By partnering with a successful organization, we can take advantage of compassionate capitalism, which is a business that puts people and the planet at the center of its success. This type of business model focuses on creating social and environmental benefits and economic gains. This type of business model is because all stakeholders should benefit from the success of the organization, including the employees, the environment, and the surrounding communities.

The profits generated by the organization should create positive social and environmental change, instead of just being used to increase the wealth of the business owners. For instance, TOMS Shoes operates on a one-for-one business model, where, for every pair of shoes purchased, the company donates a pair to a child in need. Such a model illustrates the direct positive impact that a business can have by investing its profits in creating social and environmental change.

United Nations Social Development Goals

The United Nations Social Development Goals are a set of international objectives created to promote global economic and social progress. They focus on issues such as poverty, inequality, human rights, gender equality, climate change, and access to quality education and health care. By setting these objectives, the United Nations is committed to reducing inequalities, increasing access to resources and services, and protecting the most vulnerable populations around the world. For instance, one of the main goals is to end poverty in all its forms everywhere by 2030, and to ensure that all people can access quality education, health care and economic opportunities regardless of their background or location. As Amit Ray, a peace activist, once said: "The role of The United Nations is to create more smiling faces and to fulfill the dreams of the innocent children of the world."

17 SDG LIST

GOAL 1: No Poverty
GOAL 2: Zero Hunger
GOAL 3: Good Health and Well-being
GOAL 4: Quality Education
GOAL 5: Gender Equality

GOAL 6: Clean Water and Sanitation

GOAL 7: Affordable and Clean Energy

GOAL 8: Decent Work and Economic Growth

GOAL 9: Industry, Innovation and Infrastructure

GOAL 10: Reduced Inequality

GOAL 11: Sustainable Cities and Communities

GOAL 12: Responsible Consumption and Production

GOAL 13: Climate Action

GOAL 14: Life Below Water

GOAL 15: Life on Land

GOAL 16: Peace and Justice Strong Institutions

GOAL 17: Partnerships to achieve the Goal

Excerpt from The Pursuit Podcast with Tel Ganesan

"We came into the world with nothing, and we will leave the world with nothing. We're only here for such a short amount of time, so challenge yourself to effect change. As Mahatma Gandhi once said: "Be the change that you wish to see in the world." We have a unique opportunity to make a lasting impact on the world, regardless of our circumstances. We may not take our possessions with us, but we can leave behind a legacy of positive change. Taking action on our dreams is essential even if

they seem far out of reach. After all, it's the small steps we take today that lead to the big changes we want to see tomorrow. It is through our individual contributions that we can create. meaningful and lasting change. We have the power to influence our communities, our countries, and the world. By setting an example for others, we can inspire and motivate others to make a difference. Even the smallest of actions can have a ripple effect and lead to great change."

You'll only fail if you don't act and keep thinking and dreaming, because day dreamers don't succeed. Dream about getting your idea, then pursue it. For instance, if you have an idea for a business, it's important to not just think about it and make plans, but to act and put those plans into motion. Action means taking risks, and without taking risks, you won't have any chance of success. Even if you fail, you will learn from it and be in a better position to try again. Action is an essential part of personal growth and development, and it's necessary if you want to achieve anything meaningful.

The Challenge

I am challenging people to become entrepreneurs and social entrepreneurs so we can create massive change through action. By creating a new generation of entrepreneurs and social entrepreneurs, we can develop innovative solutions to some of the biggest problems facing the world. Through their creativity and determination, these individuals can help to make the world a better place and have a real, tangible impact on the lives of others. We can transform our society, and by doing so, create a more equal and just world for all.

By providing resources, mentorship, and support to entrepreneurs, we can open pathways for new ideas, new technologies, and new ways of thinking. This can lead to more effective and sustainable solutions to poverty, climate change, and other global issues. By helping to create a more just and fair world we can help to create a more peaceful and prosperous future for all. To achieve this, we must invest in initiatives promoting inclusion, equity, and opportunity across all sectors of our society. For example, initiatives such as providing access to quality education, providing economic incentives for renewable energy sources, and encouraging private sector investment in underserved communities can help create a more inclusive and fair society.

I want to see these business owners and social entrepreneurs impact society through their efforts in addressing one or several components of social challenges. Social challenges including, poverty, inequality, lack of access to healthcare, environmental degradation, and inadequate education. Pursuing and living your version of the American Dream and your happiness will lead to wellness for the individual and healing for our country. Social entrepreneurs have the potential to create innovative solutions to social issues, which can lead to systemic change and greater access to resources and services for vulnerable populations. This could increase economic mobility, reduce disparities, and create healthier and more fair communities, which can contribute to a sense of personal fulfillment and collective wellbeing. By doing so, social entrepreneurs have the power to make a meaningful impact on society and improve the lives of countless individuals. For example, social entrepreneurs created the microfinance movement, which has provided small loans to entrepreneurs in developing countries, helping to lift millions of people out of poverty.

Instead of spending wasteful hours criticizing politicians on social media, it becomes an endless cycle of worry and dismay. I could better help society by using skills. Instead of being problematic, become problem solvers. We should aim to use our skills to help society instead of being part of the problem.

By redirecting our energy away from criticizing politicians and worrying over issues, we can become part of the solution. For instance, volunteer your time to help a local charity or organization, or use your skills to help someone in need.

This will not only help others, but it can also boost our own sense of satisfaction and accomplishment. We can feel proud of ourselves for impacting our communities and in the world. Plus, it gives us an opportunity to meet new people, learn new skills, and gain valuable experience.

We can transform our society, and by doing so, create a more equal and just world for all. By providing access to capital, social entrepreneurs have enabled individuals to pursue business opportunities, create jobs, and increase their incomes. This has enabled them to improve their living conditions and provide better opportunities for their children. In doing so, social entrepreneurs have empowered individuals to break the cycle of poverty, empowering them to make positive, lasting effects on their communities.

The choice is yours. Let's do this together. Dream your dream, pursue your happiness. Let's bring unity back to America and let's save democracy together. Embrace the power of unity and join forces to ensure a better future for our nation.

Together, we can protect democracy and make our dreams a reality. I'll be here for you as we live out The Pursuit.

Tel Ganesan
Serial Entrepreneur and
Global Humanitarian

About The Author Tel Ganesan

"Happiness is the window into your life. We have one life
that is too short, so we should follow our passion."
-Tel K. Ganesan

Unexpected Opportunities

The key to my success is serendipity, which has guided my life
and blessed me with serendipitous events. Some consider
serendipity to be fate. In Tamil Nadu, serendipity is also a folktale
told by traders.

This tale often speaks of luck and good fortune, highlighting pursuing opportunities and seizing the day. The story emphasizes the power of taking chances and going beyond the status quo. It teaches that sometimes it is necessary to take a risk in order to reap the rewards. It serves as a reminder that luck and good fortune are possible if one will go for it.

For example, one of the most popular stories is of a fisher who took the risk of sailing further than usual and ended up finding a large catch of fish. Mark Zuckerberg, the founder of Facebook, once said: "The biggest risk is not taking any risk. In a world that is changing, the only strategy that is guaranteed to fail is not taking risks."

I hope that, by sharing my life story, I will provide you with a road map of what to look for and what to avoid. I hope to enable you to make more informed decisions and choices in life. By giving you an overview of my successes, failures, and lessons learned, I want to provide you with a better understanding of the consequences of certain decisions and choices. This knowledge will arm you with the tools to make decisions that will lead you to a more fulfilling life.

To achieve a better life, it is the job of the truth seeker to find connections in all of life and act on them. Coincidences are guideposts on how to achieve happiness, prosperity, and health. By recognizing and acting upon the coincidences that life presents us with, we can create positive change in our lives. We can make decisions that are in line with our goals and values, which can lead to greater overall satisfaction and well-being. By utilizing the power of coincidences, we can make more informed decisions, gain clarity in our goals, and work to create a life we are proud of.I hope that, by sharing my life story, I will provide you with a road map of what to look for and what to avoid.

I believe all children are born with an internal drive and self-awareness, some more vividly than others. Even at a young age, a person has the potential to decide, form opinions, and explore their environment.

I believe all children are born with an internal drive and self-awareness, some more vividly than others. Even at a young age, a person has the potential to decide, form opinions, and explore their environment. It's true that a family can help people start out on the right path, but then the journey becomes personal. Upon leaving the nest and ventured out on my own, I contributed to the rest of my journey. A newfound appreciation for the role my family played in setting me up for success, but I also realized that the future I wanted was up to me and only me.

I could take the knowledge and experience I gained from my family, and apply it to my own life, deciding and taking action that would lead to the life I wanted. I also found that I gained confidence in myself, knowing that I could make my own decisions and create my own successes.

It is not uncommon for people to get sidetracked from their goals. Self-awareness can help restore that drive to succeed. With this newfound confidence, I was better equipped to stay focused on my goals, no matter how difficult the journey became. By becoming more self-aware, I could understand my strengths and weaknesses better. I could identify my triggers and address the issues that were causing me to stray from my goals. This allowed me to build a stronger sense of motivation and perseverance, which enabled me to stay on track and achieve my goals.

This experience is like a marathon runner putting in the time and training to ensure they are ready to take on the challenge. Through practice and dedication, they become more confident and self-aware of their abilities and are better equipped to reach their goals despite the difficulties they may face.

Land of the Holy

People always ask me how I could grow up in the Tiruchirappalli region of southern India and become a global millionaire in a couple of decades. It was no easy feat, but with hard work and dedication to my craft, I could achieve success beyond my wildest dreams. I worked hard to build a business empire that spanned multiple countries and industries. I leveraged my business acumen and knowledge of the global market to identify lucrative opportunities and capitalized on them, resulting in significant financial gains. As the famous Indian entrepreneur, Dr Roopleen once said: "If you have a dream, don't just sit there. Believe in yourself and work hard to make your dreams come true.

There are three of India's holiest temples in my hometown of Trichy, which is an   ancient city in the Tamil Nadu region. It is the Mecca of Hindu practice. Serendipity   remains one of life's most valuable values, despite the repeated retelling of the Tamil Nadu Traders' story for thousands of years. The repeated repetition of the Tamil Nadu Traders story for thousands of years, serendipity remains one of life's most valuable values. Thus, the tales of serendipity, along with the holy temples, are a reminder of recognizing and appreciating the beauty of life in its most basic form.

The traders of Tamil Nadu have a long tradition of storytelling and this folk tale of serendipity is a prime example. It is a reminder to be open to the surprises and unexpected blessings that life can bring. We should cherish and celebrate these moments that come as a surprise and unplanned. English writer and politician Horace Walpole coined the word serendipity in 1754 based on the Persian story of The Three Princes of Serendip.

In the story, the princes were always making discoveries by accident, which Walpole thought of as serendipity. He derived the word from the Persian phrase "Sarandip," which was the old name of the Tiruchirappalli region of southern India.

As the famous author Roy T. Bennett once wrote: "When you open your mind, you open new doors to new possibilities for yourself and new opportunities to help others." So, if you ever feel like they have presented you with a once-in-a-lifetime opportunity, just think of the Tamil Nadu traders and seize the moment! After all, it's not every day you have time to make a fortune selling coconuts!

I had a joyous upbringing in the city of Tiruchirapalli, India, which is renowned as the Holy City, with a lot of ancient temples dating back over 1500 years. Being a tourist destination, people from various places often frequented it. There were many Temples, as well as a significant number of Churches and Mosques, and there was a unity in diversity. It had once been a British colony, so my city had excellent hospitals and educational institutions that the missionaries had built. As a result, we had easy access to good health and education.

Holidays were always a special time, when I would spend count-less hours with my cousins and friends.

I used to wander around the long corridors and prayer halls in the temples, marveling at the fitted carved stone pillars. During my childhood, I also remember gazing at the tourists, imaging where they had traveled from. There were many festivals, temple carnivals, and celebrations, and I remember where everyone in my family would assemble to celebrate. My mother was a fortunate woman and there were always a lot of guests. She spread her positivity to everyone who visited our house. She was keen on sending us to Catholic schools that emphasized discipline and language training. My father worked at a well known bank, and I always remember him as a courageous man. I share a lot of wonderful memories with my younger brother and my sister. Today, we all work together at Kyyba, where I feel gratified and happy to be around the people with whom I can love, trust, and share my knowledge.

Land of the Free

Since I was a child, I have grown to know that the USA is the greatest democracy in the world, the land of the free. Freedom comes with a lot of responsibilities, and only when I was ready to take those responsibilities could I truly enjoy it. The freedom that comes with being a citizen of the USA gives individuals the power to make choices and pursue their dreams, something that many people in the world cannot do. It also comes with the responsibility of upholding the values of democracy, such as justice and equality, and being an active member of the community. With this responsibility comes the power to make a meaningful difference in the lives of those who are less fortunate.

Students from India have formed a golden highway between the motherland and the United States. Over 25 million Indians live abroad. Because of the increasing number of Indian students that are applying to, and attending, universities in the United States.

The economic growth in India has led to increased demand for skilled labor. The highway has become even more pronounced as the number of successful Indian individuals and businesses in the United States has grown, further reinforcing the idea that the United States provides a great opportunity for Indians to pursue their dreams. For example, Indian-born entrepreneurs and innovators in the United States such as Google's Sundar Pichai, Satya Nadella of Microsoft, and Shantanu Narayen of Adobe, have become household names in India and have inspired generations Indian students to pursue education and careers in the United States.

I estimate that 2.6 million of them live in the United States, making it the third largest immigrant group. Most students who come to America to study engineering. Among the reasons, according to researchers Rahul Choudaha and Megha Roy, is the economic connection to the U.S. market to engineer and information technology. Even more remarkable is that many of these immigrants not only come to the U.S. to pursue an engineering career, but often gain success and recognition in their chosen field. The range of opportunities in the U.S. for engineers is extensive, allowing immigrants to find a range of roles and levels of responsibility. Combined with availability funding, the U.S. is a popular destination for engineering study and employment. The U.S. is well-known for its commitment to research, innovation and technology, making it an attractive place for engineers to come and develop their skills.

American TV and the possibility of succeeding in the world's most powerful country fascinated students. They dreamed of one day making it there and achieving the same success as their idols. This combines the idea of the American Dream and the glamorization of American culture in the media.

These images of wealth and success were appealing to students who were looking for a way to make their own dreams come true.

The reason engineering is so prized is that after India achieved its independence from the British in 1947, creating a democratic nation became a mission. India gained its independence from the British on August 15, 1947. This mission required a new generation of engineers who could help build the infrastructure, communications networks, and industry the country needed to become a modern nation. I saw engineering as the key to India's economic development, and so it was a field that was invested in and valued. To further this goal, the Indian government began offering engineering scholarships to the best and brightest students across the country, providing them with the opportunity to gain the skills and knowledge necessary to contribute to the nation's progress.

The Indian economy has grown thanks to the use of information technology, civil engineering, and software analysis. Bachelors who have steady employment are more likely to marry. The 2,000-year-old caste system is loosening some of its grip, but both in India and America, we still have a lot to do. With the influx of educated and employed bachelors, the stigma of inter-caste marriages has lessened and is becoming more acceptable. However, there are still many issues that need to be addressed, such as the gender pay gap, the lack of access to education, and the lack of representation in the workplace. To move towards a fairer society, we must continue to confront these issues and strive for equal opportunity for all, regardless of caste, gender, or socioeconomic background.

Being a citizen of two worlds allows me to concentrate on projects that benefit humanity and raise funds needed to do so. My Indian heritage grounds and focuses my thoughts.

This combination of global and local perspectives makes me qualified to create meaningful change in the world. I understand the need for both large-scale solutions that can affect a large population, and localized solutions that can help individual communities. I can use my understanding of both worlds to create impactful initiatives that are both effective and sustainable. It's like a pilot using the navigation systems on a plane to figure out where they are now and how to reach their desired destination.

By combining their local knowledge with a larger perspective, they can create a safe, efficient flight plan that maximizes their impact.

I find the greatest rush in life is doing things others won't do. Except bungee jumping. I draw the line there. Taking risks is an essential part of growing and pushing the boundaries of what's possible. By taking risks, you can gain a better understanding of yourself and the world around you. It also helps to build confidence, resilience and can even lead to personal growth and development. Taking risks can also be a service to others. When we take risks, we can be a role model to others, inspiring them to step outside of their comfort zone and take risks of their own. Taking risks can also lead to new opportunities and create a ripple effect of good in the world.

East Meets West

Culture plays a crucial role in our lives and because of this, it becomes very significant that we learn to adapt. When two different cultures come together, each brings with it different values, beliefs, and customs.

Learning to understand and appreciate the differences between cultures is the key to successful interactions. It can also lead to better global understanding and peace. To foster a positive and peaceful environment, it is important to become familiar with different cultures and learn to appreciate the unique perspectives they bring. By doing so, we can create a more united world and better global relationships.

There are enormous differences between India and the United States of America. These differences can range from the way each country approaches religion, to the way they view education, to the way they handle their economy. Learning to accept and appreciate these differences can help to create a more unified world and foster positive relationships between the two countries. Both India and the United States of America have a unique heritage and a unique set of values that shape their respective cultures. By taking the time to learn about and embrace cultural differences, we can move towards a more interconnected and harmonious future.

Eastern philosophy influences the philosophy of India, for example: Respect: In India, respect means not saying anything, but in the United States, we can see it as a sign of failure if you say nothing. People from India face this fundamental issue when they move to a new country like America. It is the idea of respect itself that is at the core of the issue.

The secret to my recipe is to blend the best of both east and west cultures. Respect for different cultures is paramount for achieving harmony and balance in life.

With the help of both eastern and western business principles, I was able to transform my career into a more advantageous one. By bridging cultures and understanding the values of both sides, I was able to maximize my potential and make a successful career transition. By combining the efficiency of western business practices with the holistic approach of eastern philosophies, I was able to create a unique approach to my work. This enabled me to focus on the big picture and think outside the box, helping me to reach a level of success that I would not have been able to achieve by using one system alone.

Spirituality and Serendipity: In eastern culture, there is an emphasis on connecting with your spirituality and soul, but in America, the primary focus is getting settled into a career. The eastern culture goes with the flow and solves problems for the entire group. Eastern culture values collective harmony over individual success and the   belief that the whole is greater than the sum of its parts. As a result, eastern cultures focus more on cooperative problem-solving and conflict resolution strategies. Western culture encourages an individualistic approach to problem-solving and   conflict resolution, where the focus is on achieving individual success, rather than   focusing on collective harmony.

In most Asian and Middle Eastern countries, however, forthrightness is rude. Instead, indirectness is the preferred way of expressing oneself in these cultures. It's all about ME, ME, ME in Western culture. It's all about oneself, not anyone else. The reason ME is so important here is clear to me. You cannot succeed if you lack confidence and strength. As a contrast, the east places so much emphasis on family, the environment, and all outer boundaries that they live for others rather than for themselves.

We live for ourselves in America, and family is part of who we are, but not what we revolve around. In the east, family and community are much more important than individualism, so they often focus their lives on taking care of their loved ones and contributing to their community. Americans focus more on individual success and achieving their own goals, rather than on the collective good. As a result, Americans strive for self-fulfillment, whereas Eastern cultures place more emphasis on the collective well-being of their family and community.

With the GoGoGo attitude, I have been able to maintain those vibes of selflessness, kindness, and caring for others. It has allowed me to remain focused on giving back to the community, dedicating my efforts to help those in need.

America is a country where anyone can pursue their dreams, and that is what I love about it. Working hard and learning my boundaries keeps me motivated. Regardless of where anyone lives, they can maintain their identity while adopting successful elements that work elsewhere. With hard work, I can identify both my strengths and weaknesses, which drive me to succeed. By understanding my context, I can adapt useful concepts from other areas in order to maintain my unique identity.

Land of Opportunity

"How people treat you is their karma; how you react is yours."
-Dr. Wayne Dyer

After graduating, I would begin my job search. I couldn't wait to prove my worth to a company that would keep me in America.

Securing a job in the US would be my chance to show the knowledge and skills I gained during my studies - and the start of an exciting new chapter of my life. With my degree in hand, I knew I could matter. I wanted to use my knowledge to be a part of something meaningful and help make a positive impact on the world. I knew I could show potential employers the value I could bring to their organization.

The search for a job was a full-time job for me since I had one year before my foreign student visa expired. My abiding goal was to become an automotive engineer, so I devoted myself to learning math and science. I attended workshops, seminars and conferences on the subject, studied technical manuals, and volunteered in engineering firms to gain insight into the profession. Networking opportunities allowed me to meet engineers, build relationships, and gain industry-specific knowledge. I leveraged the relationships I developed to gain access to information that wasn't available to the public, and this helped me to land my dream job.

As a recent immigrant, I developed an interesting mindset while searching for jobs. Some days, I felt like a yogi in a Trichy temple, breathing in the energy of peace. Sometimes I was like Stephen Jobs, who founded Apple Computer, or George Lucas, who created the Star Wars franchise, creating products and inspiring people around the world beyond what humanity has ever imagined.

Blending cultures and creating a place here have always been my goals. For example, I have blended my cultural knowledge and experiences to create a series of events that celebrate diversity and inclusion within my community.

I needed to improve my ability to speak up and promote my talents. In India, they   discourage this. Even though the country is a democracy, criticizing the government unadvisable. They have banned government critics from some of India's 45 central universities. Publishers resist printing material that incurs the wrath of the right-wing ruling establishment. Students do not blame their teachers in public. Students must study. It was a good discipline to bring to America. I realized I needed to change my mindset and be more assertive in my communication. This was difficult to do in India, given the societal norms and expectations of obedience to authority figures. In   America, however, I found an environment of open discussion and debate that I could use to practice my newfound assertiveness. I adapted to this new freedom and found that I could express myself more confidently. This gave me the courage to take on more leadership roles and challenge my teachers without fear of repercussions.

When I was in college, my classmates taught me how important making connections. If there was a field trip to an automotive plant, I jumped on it. I would get an automotive executive's name and phone number and call him to get advice on programs that would be job magnets soon. By doing this, I could get an inside look into the industry and find out what skills were most valuable in the job market. This enabled me to tailor my studies to increase my chances of getting a job in the automotive industry. It also gave me initiative in my job search, giving me an advantage over my coworkers.

After a few spectacular failures, I learned how to get through school, made lasting friends, and got jobs. It is my recommendation that young people join student organizations, volunteer for projects they, and attend conventions to land their first job. By doing this, they will gain valuable experience, build a network of contacts, and develop the skills they need to succeed in their   chosen field. Not only will these activities help them build the skills they need to succeed, but they will also provide invaluable networking opportunities. This will allow them to meet potential employers and learn about opportunities in their field. In addition, these activities will help them develop a sense of purpose and confidence that will help them succeed in their chosen field.

To help students and young professionals network with global entrepreneurs, I helped start the Michigan chapter of TiE, the Talent, Ideas and Entrepreneurship organization. In the Michigan chapter of TiE, I have strived to provide students and young professionals with the opportunity to forge meaningful relationships with the world's most influential entrepreneurs. Through this organization, I have been able to connect students and young professionals to successful entrepreneurs and help them learn and gain valuable insights into the field of entrepreneurship. This has enabled them to gain invaluable knowledge and experience that can help them in their own business endeavors.

Driven By Dreams

I say that no matter where you come from, your dreams are valid. You can bring them to life. If you work for them, dreams can become reality.

No matter if you are an engineer, or any other profession, no dream is too big if you put in the effort and strive for it. Everyone has the potential to reach their goals and make their dreams come true, regardless of their career path. With dedicated work, dedication, and a positive attitude, anyone can make their dreams a reality.

Although I studied at the University of Oklahoma, I wanted to study car production, so I transferred to Wayne State University in Detroit. It was before the millennials flooded the city, and I worked at a campus for Burger King, flipping burgers. A menial job cannot spark the drive to study and succeed. The job gave me the financial stability to pursue my studies, but it did not give me the motivation to do so. My ambition to learn more about car production kept me motivated and allowed me to transfer to a university that specialized in it. I reignited my passion for cars and pursued the career I had always dreamed of.

The field of mechanical engineering intrigued me because I could study vehicle emissions, assembly plants, automobile safety, or even autonomous vehicles. Wayne's professors taught advanced problem-solving skills that would help in any endeavor. I delighted my father that I chose the car industry for my paychecks. It employs more than a million people in America, not including dealerships and aftermarket services. Mechanical engineering also offers the opportunity to explore innovative solutions to the world's energy and environmental challenges. Through research and development, engineers can create technologies that reduce emissions, increase efficiency, and improve safety for many vehicles. Projections show the field will grow faster than the average for all occupations, making it a desirable, rewarding career choice.

With the right knowledge and skills, mechanical engineers have the potential to make a positive impact on the world and to build a successful, stable career.

I graduated from Wayne State University in 1989 with a degree in engineering. I joined Chrysler. In 2005, after I followed my dream to start Kyyba Inc., a staffing services company, the Great Recession struck, affecting the automotive industry and much of Kyyba's business. As a result, Kyyba diversified into other industries, which set the stage for continued growth. I was determined to ensure Kyyba's success and built a foundation that enabled our future expansion.

When I return home on business, I am overwhelmed by the progress engineers have made in building dreams. Human ingenuity has helped bring us to this point. We have achieved remarkable advances in technology in such a short amount of time. Amazing to consider that what I once considered science fiction is now reality.   Technologies such as artificial intelligence, virtual reality, and robotics have become commonplace and continue to improve our lives in ways we never imagined. The   future holds even greater possibilities, and it's exciting to consider what new heights humanity will reach.

Many people are already coming into and out of India, especially for the movie industry, before construction has even begun. The airports cannot accommodate all the people coming into and out of India. We limit the existing airports in terms of their size and capacity. As more people come into and out of India, the airports will become congested, resulting in delays and cancellations. To ease this issue, existing airports need to be modernized and ex-panded to increase capacity, while new airports will need to be constructed to keep up with the growing demand.

Several international automakers build cars here, including Fiat Chrysler, BMW, Honda, and Mercedes Benz. Immigrants are instrumental to the success of these. Without their hard work, dedication, and innovation, these multinational corporations would not be as successful as they are.

Immigrants often take on the more difficult and tedious jobs in the auto industry, such as assembly line work, which can be hazardous and require long hours.

Their technical expertise and diverse cultural perspectives have helped to create new products and improving existing ones.

Today, my company, Kyyba, has over 700 employees and millions in revenue, makes me a folk hero. Even in a climate where they hold immigrants, where people fear   foreigners taking their jobs away, I've been a job incubator in movies, information technology, smart phone apps and autonomous vehicles.

My success story has been an inspiration for many, showing them that with hard work, persistence, and dedication, anyone can reach their dreams, regardless of their   origin. This success has brought a sense of hope to people who felt like it has left   behind them in the digital age, where new technology and global competition have disrupted many traditional job opportunities. My story shows that there are still paths to success and that anyone, regardless of their background, can reach their goals. As the famous Indian doctor Roopleen once said: "If you have a dream, don't just sit there. Believe that you can achieve success and do everything you can to make it a reality.

Although I wanted action, I had to hold back my dreams and manage my disappointments. It was difficult.

So I kept reminding myself of the saying, "Where there is a will, there is a way." This became my mantra, and I was determined to make my dreams come true. I knew that if I focused on the end goal, I could stay motivated and put in the hard work necessary to make it happen. I was determined to make my dreams a reality, no matter the obstacles I faced. So I kept telling myself, "If I can't find a way, I'll make one!"

I used Kyyba as a springboard for other business ventures, like Kyyba Innovations, Kyyba Wellness, Kyyba Music, and Kyyba Films, which have even expanded into film production. Kyyba Kidz Foundation provides job skills to the most deprived children, and I am also the founder.

Over the years, I know the USA is the greatest democracy in the world, the land of the free. With freedom comes a lot of responsibility and only when I was ready to take on that responsibility and do the right things for society could I enjoy its freedom. By assuming and exercising my responsibility, I have grown to understand and appreciate the freedoms that the USA offers more deeply, making it the most rewarding democracy in the world. Thus, I understand and appreciate the freedoms that the USA offers, and in doing so, I have gained an even greater appreciation of the nation's status as the greatest democracy in the world.

Mentor

In 2016, I stepped back to the chair role at Kyyba and made helping other entrepreneurs a priority. I wanted to provide guidance and mentorship to those   starting their own journey, and to shape the next generation of successful business leaders. I founded Kyyba Innovations, which runs competitions such as the Pitch Club MI and Detroit FinTech Challenge to promote disruption in the latest technologies and drive innovation. I'm passionate about creating opportunities for entrepreneurs and innovators to showcase their ideas and make a meaningful impact on the world.

The Pitch Club Format is a shining example of how to bring together and promote local and statewide business ecosystems. By enabling networking, connecting ideas, resources, and fostering collaboration, Pitch Club Format has become an invaluable part of many entrepreneurs' success stories.

Part of my mission is to bring the Pitch Club Format to every state in the nation to   invigorate ecosystems on a national level. I'm confident that I can achieve this goal and am looking forward to a future of abundant resources for entrepreneurs of all backgrounds.

Motivational Speaker

Public speaking is something I enjoy doing. Striving to use my passion for public speaking to help others reach their goals. Everyone has the potential to achieve their dreams, and I use my public speaking skills to help people recognize and realize their potential. I also use my platform to motivate and inspire people to take action and reach their goals.

In addition, one of my passions is seed funding initiatives I believe in. By doing this, I'm able to help bring others 'dreams to life, while also supporting innovative projects that I am passionate about. Seed funding is a way to help entrepreneurs and other innovators get their projects off the ground, while also allowing me to be a part of something bigger than myself. It's a way to make a difference in the world while also supporting projects I believe in.

Since 2009, I have been the President of TiE Detroit, an organization founded to   promote U.S.-Indian trade. During my second term as president of The Indus Entrepreneurs (TiE) Detroit chapter (2016-2018), I chaired five mega annual conferences (TiECONs) over two consecutive years.

Movie Producer

Film and art have always been a passion for me. As I have grown older, I have appreciated the power of a good story in both film and art, and strive to create pieces that evoke emotion in viewers. This appreciation for storytelling has only grown with time, as I recognize the power of art in communicating ideas, feelings, and perspectives. I strive to create works that communicate something meaningful to its viewers, whether it be a thought-provoking message or an emotional experience.

I feel proud that I'm contributing to the creation of more films. It is a great honor to be part of something so beneficial to the world. In this way, I hope to make a lasting impact on my audience, one that will leave them with a lasting impression of my work.

My enthusiasm for filmmaking is only growing as I continue to explore the craft of storytelling and bring my own visions to life. I am refining my skills in order to deliver the most impactful stories possible and bring to life my creative vision.

I'm eager to see where this journey leads me, and I'm confident that I can use my unique perspective to create something special. With this end goal in mind, I am honing my skills and pushing the boundaries of storytelling to capture the essence of my creative vision. I am eager to see the possibilities that lie ahead and am certain my unique approach will allow me to create something remarkable.

Podcaster

Podcasting has been a great experience for me. It has helped me to connect with people from around the world and share my ideas. By having a podcast, I am able to reach a wide audience and it has allowed me to have meaningful conversations with people from different countries and cultures. I have also been able to share my thoughts and experiences with people who may not have access to the same opportunities as I do.

The podcasting medium allows me to pursue my passions while also involving guests. Podcasting allows for a more intimate exchange of ideas than other mediums such as radio or television. It also allows for a more flexible format, which allows for a wide range of topics to be discussed.
By having guests it adds an element of collaboration and exchange that can be rewarding.

Also, podcasting allows me to explore and share ideas with others in a way that is both engaging and educational.

Checkout **The Pursuit** Podcast at:

www.theamericandreamguru.com

Philanthropist

Whenever and however I can, I try to make the world a better place than it already is by helping those in need. Whether it be donating to a charity, volunteering my time to an organization, or giving advice and support to someone in need, I believe it is my responsibility as a human being to help create a better world. I believe it is a duty to use the resources available to me to help make a positive impact on the world and to contribute to the greater good.

Besides feeling positive about myself, doing my part helps me feel like I am doing something that matters. By engaging in activities that benefit the world, I contribute to the cause of making the world a better place. I know even the smallest gestures of kindness and care can have a lasting effect on someone's life. Therefore, I strive to be conscious of each interaction I have and to make sure I am creating positive change.

Checkout and follow **Kyyba Kids Foundation**:

www.kyybakidzfoundation.org

PHOTO GALLERY

END NOTES

Additional Dedication to: **Meghann Mealbach**

"Meghann was a young filmmaker that worked many of my events, and created hundreds of marketing videos for all my endeavors. She even spearheaded an Internet Cooking Show for me. We lost Meghann to breast cancer, but her passion and creativity live on in our hearts and minds. Meg's Nonprofit created to honor her memory will be assisting in our social impact challenge. It's called ***Meg's Missions LLC."***

Chapter 1   THE MISSION

1. Excerpt from "The Pursuit" Podcast with Tel Ganesan Copyright Tel Ganesan 2022

Chapter 2   DIVIDED NATION

Chapter 3   AMERICAN DREAM

1. Excerpt from "The Pursuit" Podcast with Tel Ganesan Copyright Tel Ganesan 2022
2. Excerpt from "The Pursuit" Podcast with Tel Ganesan Copyright Tel Ganesan 2022
3. The Global Millionaire Magazine Cover August 2022

Chapter 4   ENTREPRENEURSHIP

1. Excerpt from "The Pursuit" Podcast with Tel Ganesan Copyright Tel Ganesan 2022
2. Excerpt from "The Pursuit" Podcast with Tel Ganesan Copyright Tel Ganesan 2022

3. Excerpt from "The Pursuit" Podcast with Tel Ganesan Copyright Tel Ganesan 2022

Chapter 5   MASSIVE SOCIAL IMPACT

1. Excerpt from "The Pursuit" Podcast with Tel Ganesan Copyright Tel Ganesan 2022

Chapter 6   ABOUT THE AUTHOR

1. Article about Tel Ganesan Website: **Dreams are for Real**, Latestly.com

2. Article about Tel Ganesan Website: **I am Living Proof of the American Dream**, by Chef Vicky Colas, Authority Magazine

3. Article about Tel Ganesan Website: **Driving Entrepreneurship**, ValiantCEO.com

Tel Ganesan can be found at:

www.theamericandreamguru.com

Tel's website: www.telkganesan.com
Facebook at: www.facebook.com/telkg
Instagram at: www.instagram.com/telkganesan
Linked In, connect with me at www.linkedin.com/in/telkganesan
Twitter, you can follow me at @Telganesan

Tel Ganesan Imdb: www.imdb.com/name/nm9102200/

PARTING NOTE

"Thank you for reading The Pursuit.
We are all the authors of our lives. Let's manifest happiness into
your life. Let's be the difference we want to see in others!"

Tel Ganesan
The American Dream Guru
www.theamericandreamguru.com

CPSIA information can be obtained
at www.ICGtesting.com
Printed in the USA
BVHW072207040423
661733BV00012B/331